STEPS AND STAGES: FROM 6 TO 8

The Early School Years

Holly Bennett and Teresa Pitman

KEY PORTER BOOKS

Canadian Cataloguing in Publication Data

Pitman, Teresa
    Steps & stages 6-8: the school years

(Steps & stages guides)
ISBN 1-55013-974-6

1. School children. 2. Child development. 3. Child rearing. I. Bennett, Holly, 1957- . II. Title. III. Title: steps and stages six to eight. IV. Series: Pitman, Teresa. Steps & stages guides.

HQ769.B577   1998   649'.124   C97-932793-8

The publisher gratefully acknowledges the support of the Canada Council for the Arts and the Ontario Arts Council for its publishing program.

THE CANADA COUNCIL | LE CONSEIL DES ARTS
FOR THE ARTS | DU CANADA
SINCE 1957 | DEPUIS 1957

Key Porter Books Limited
70 The Esplanade
Toronto, Ontario
Canada M5E 1R2

www.keyporter.com

Electronic formatting: Jean Lightfoot Peters

Printed and bound in Canada

98 99 00 01 6 5 4 3 2 1

Contents

Acknowledgements

AS ALWAYS, OUR THANKS MUST GO FIRST TO THE PARENTS and professionals who have been so generous with their time, thoughtful about our questions, and honest in sharing their experiences with children.

To Bonny Reichert and our other editors, past and present, at *Today's Parent*, and to our Key Porter editor Barbara Berson, who handled the sticky business of editing an editor with grace and helped us turn a motley collection of columns into a series of real books.

To Holly's husband, John Hoffman—an inspiring father, ever-supportive partner, and all-round Renaissance guy.

And last, but not least, to the kids—ours and everyone else's—who help us grow as parents and as people.

First Words

THESE ARE THE YEARS OF BIKES AND BEST FRIENDS, soccer and Sega, and learning about the world both at home and at school. Your six- to eight-year-old is still young enough to greet you with a hug and a kiss, but old enough to forbid you to do it in front of the whole class. He may be playing with building blocks one minute and mastering a complicated computer game the next. He is becoming more competent every day: learning to skate, to read, to hold his own in the schoolyard, to count his own money.

It's true that your child's development is less spectacular at this stage than in the preschool years, but it's no less challenging. Reasoning, social skills, physical abilities, moral judgement: all are becoming increasingly sophisticated. While many children are exuberantly cheerful and easy to get along with during these early school years, others find them a tough transition. Some don't like school or have trouble making friends; some worry, some daydream, and some just can't sit still.

Not all kids are interested in the clubs and sports that many join at this age, but their parents are kept pretty busy all the same. For some, these years are a whirlwind of activity: parent council meetings, field trips, and class bake sales; Beavers, music lessons, gymnastics, and sleepovers. After all that, who has time to just relax with their kids? You might have to actually schedule that in, too—because having an hour or two to talk, read together, play catch, or go for a walk is crit-

ical to maintaining that strong relationship with your child that you
have worked so hard to build.

Holly Bennett   *Teresa Pitman*

LIVING TOGETHER
Between Parent and Child

"IT GETS EASIER ONCE THEY'RE PAST the preschool years, right?" one father (trying, as he spoke, to calm a toddler's raging temper tantrum) asked another. The second father, whose children were older, laughed. "Not easier, just different."

Children in this age group are not so prone to temper tantrums, and the skills of toilet-training and going to bed alone have probably been mastered. But there are new responsibilities for your child to learn, and new ways for you to relate. The persuasive techniques that worked with a four-year-old are no longer so effective. These kids are ready to negotiate with you, and they are acutely aware of issues of fairness and justice.

Some of the changes may surprise you. The toddler who doffed her clothes whenever your back was turned and delighted in running around "all bare" is now the seven-year-old who insists on total privacy whenever she changes or uses the bathroom. Your non-stop five-year-old chatterer may now answer your question, "How was school today?" with a cursory "Okay"—if he answers at all. And if she ever thought you were the fountain of all wisdom, she's likely to change her mind in the coming years, as she develops her own strong ideas about how things should be done.

These changes are all part of the growing-up process. While home and family are still really important, your child is figuring out who he is and how he fits into the wider world of school, neighbourhood, and community.

"CAN WE TALK?" HELPING KIDS SHARE WHAT'S ON THEIR MIND

he year my son turned six, his best friend was in his class, and life was good—until one day his friend stayed home sick. He was very upset, and after crying for a bit, spent the morning at school drifting around forlornly by himself. At least, that's how his teacher described it.

So, over lunch, I did my tactful best to help him tell me about it.

"How was school today, honey?"

"Great!" came the hearty reply. OK, I asked for that. Try again.

"I guess you probably missed having Joe to play with."

"No." (This in a tone of puzzled scorn.) "There's lots of other kids to play with."

We don't always run into such a brick wall with our kids, but children in this age group can have a lot on their minds—and it's not always easy for them to put it into words.

Child psychiatrist and mother Joanna Santa Barbara comments: "This is an age where there are a number of new realizations, some of them quite momentous. For example, children are beginning to perceive themselves in a social context, to become concerned about how others see them and to compare themselves to others. That can be difficult, especially for kids who have learning disabilities, or less mature social skills, or a physical characteristic like obesity that makes them stand out.

"At the same time," says Santa Barbara, "they don't have a tremendously well-developed vocabulary to talk about their feelings."

How can parents help kids open up about what's on their minds? Santa Barbara suggests that specific "listening techniques" are less important than the everyday climate in the family.

"It starts with a family framework of values and practices that respect people's feelings and encourage communication," she says. "Can the adults express themselves openly, show affection, talk about their good and bad feelings, work through problems together? Do the parents listen to the children?"

It seems obvious that kids who know they can count on a receptive ear are more likely to open up to us when they are troubled. The problem is, parents and kids don't always want to talk about the same things. As Ron Taffel, author of *Parenting by Heart*, acknowledges bluntly, "A lot of what kids have to say is *boring* to parents!" Do you really want to know where all the secrets are in *The Legend of Zelda*, or what happened on a *Full House* rerun? But as Santa Barbara says, "It's an issue of respect. They're telling you because there's something there that is important to them." So when we can make the effort—most of the time—to listen when our kids share their interests, they may be more likely to come to us with more complicated feelings.

What if we can see our child is troubled, but she doesn't come to us? Sometimes all it takes, says Santa Barbara, is to share our observation: "You look sad" or "You're very quiet today." We might even take a stab at what we think the problem is—especially if it's likely to be difficult for the child to blurt it out: "I know you were looking forward to being with your dad this weekend, and then he had to cancel. I wonder if that's what's upsetting you?" Sometimes kids need help finding the words to describe their mixed-up feelings, or reassurance that it's okay to "let them out."

School-aged children are developing a sense of self-consciousness, a capacity for embarrassment, and a need for some privacy. All these factors can make a child suddenly touchy about being questioned, or just generally less forthcoming.

"There are many kids who feel pressured and put on the spot to 'produce' when we sit them down to have the Talk," says Santa Barbara.

4

TALKING GAMES: BREAKING THE ICE

One way to expand our conversational possibilities with kids is to play "talking games"—they help us break out of the "what-did-you-do-today?" rut and get to know more about each other. These are good for long car drives, short bedtime chats, or the dinner table. For starters:

- Name your favourite animal, game, or TV show.
- List foods, colours, sports you like and dislike.
- Ask, what would you rather be, a zebra or a car? A tree or a rock?
- If you had to be a different age, how old would you want to be?
- If you had to live in one of your friends' families, which would you pick?
- Were you sad, glad, mad, or bad today? Why? Take turns with each one.

Sharing memories is another way to encourage trust and sharing. Children love to hear stories of their parents' childhood, and it's reassuring for them to realize that you had difficult times, too: "I remember when I was in grade one, and the teacher wouldn't let me go to the washroom. I wet my pants, and I was so embarrassed I started crying." You can exchange memories with each other: What's a good memory from our vacation last year? What do you remember about Christmas when you were really little? Remember when Snuff was just a puppy, how he got stuck under the back porch?

"It's often easier if you join the child in his play or some other activity, and play and talk at the same time."

Taffel calls this "parallel conversation": "Think about the best conversations you've ever had with your child. Chances are, they've been talks you didn't *engineer*. They just 'happened'—while driving, walking to the school bus, doing the laundry, tucking your child into bed. You probably weren't even looking directly at each other."

So if your child tends to be close-mouthed, you might create more opportunities for these "casual" conversations—play a board game, make a salad together, linger after lights-out. It just may give her the time and space she needs to share her exciting breakthrough in reading, her desire to make friends with a new classmate, her humiliation in the lunch room, or her confusion about sex.

And what about my Mr. Denial, and his "great" school day? It could be, says Santa Barbara, that my son wanted to handle this problem himself. Sometimes we just have to respect that, unless we see that the child is really not able to cope on his own. But she suggests a nice way of offering support, without putting him on the spot: "It seems that having your friend away must have been hard for you and you must have missed him, but I also know that you're learning to manage on your own."

I'd like another crack at that conversation. I think what I really said was, "Oh. Want some more milk?"

TRY AND TRY AGAIN: LEARNING TO PERSEVERE

S even-year-old Katie is in the backyard, playing catch with her mom. She misses her first three catches, and throws her mitt down in disgust. "It's OK, Kate, you'll get the hang of it," encourages her mother. "Try holding your other hand over the glove, like this, so you can trap the ball when it lands." Katie gives it one more half-hearted attempt. But when she misses again, she's gone. "I don't like this game," she mutters. "I'm gonna watch TV."

Jeff is doing his grade-three math homework. "It's too hard! I can't do it," he announces. "Let's see, Jeff," says his dad. "What part are you having trouble with?"

"All of it!"

"Well, let's take the first problem. How would you start?"

"I don't know! It's stupid, and I'm not doing it!" Jeff slams his book shut and runs, crying, up to his room.

Whatever happened to "try and try again?" It's not dead—you don't have to look far to find kids who are working hard to master hockey skills or whistling or the next level of Donkey Kong. But persistence and effort in the face of difficulty does not come easily to many children, and if it seems to you that your kids don't "stick with it" as well as you did at that age, you may be right.

Harvey Mandel, a psychology professor at York University in Toronto, says, "Many kids do have unrealistic expectations today. We live in a world that is intolerant of process. There's instant everything—instant communication, instant TV images, instant food, instant sports stars. Kids see the finished product, but not what leads up to it. They don't realize, for example, how many years of practice go into becoming a professional athlete."

Ester Cole, a supervising psychologist with the Toronto Board of

Education, adds that the very pace of life today rushes children to focus on end results, rather than the learning process. "Many parents are hurried themselves because of their work and lifestyle. It's difficult to allow your child the time to struggle with her shoelaces when it's holding up the whole family." But in the end, she muses, we may be giving kids the message that achievement should come easily. "We tend to give appreciation for the ability to do or learn things quickly, and not so much for effort."

Is this a problem? Well, yes. For one thing, people who always want to leapfrog to the final gate won't, in the end, achieve as well—even if they're talented and bright. The ability to stay with a task, and tolerate initial failures without discouragement, is unlikely to become an obsolete life skill no matter how quickly the world turns.

There's something else. Children who haven't learned to "try and try again" are, as they get older, at risk of developing a "helpless" self-image. In his book *The Optimistic Child*, Martin Seligman explains it this way: "In order for your child to experience mastery, it is necessary for him to fail, to feel bad, and to try again repeatedly until success occurs. None of these steps can be circumvented. Failure and feeling bad are necessary building blocks for ultimate success and feeling good."

A child (or adult) who adopts a pattern of abandoning difficult tasks in order to avoid frustration is at risk of "learned helplessness," warns Seligman. In effect, he deprives himself of success and misses out on the experiences that would build confidence in his own abilities. By contrast, the child who keeps trying, and succeeds, is learning that "I can."

So how can we help our kids develop an "I can" attitude?

Break up challenges into "small, surmountable steps" so they seem less overwhelming, says Cole. "When a child says, 'I'm not good at math,' help him be more specific. Often it's only a small area of difficulty." Similarly, a young child who sets his sights on being a concert pianist is likely to become discouraged long before he has a chance to experience that important sense of mastery. A good teacher will find

QUESTIONS ABOUT QUITTING

And now the tough question: If it's good to encourage children to keep trying, should we also forbid them to quit? Make them keep on with piano lessons, assign them an hour of skating practice every weekend?

Sometimes a parent can see that the child is "nearly there," and just needs a gentle push to experience the rewards of extra effort. But, cautions Cole, "You don't want to turn this into a power struggle. There you have the potential for doing more harm than good."

That doesn't mean you can't insist that she complete a chore properly, or finish her homework. Of course you can—that's part of learning about responsibility. And when it comes to organized activities, it's reasonable to expect kids to give a new activity "a fair try." Explain to your child that the first attempts at a new sport or skill can be frustrating, and she needs to stick with it long enough to see what it's really like. That might be a few sessions, one series of lessons, or a sports season, depending on the age and temperament of your child and the activity involved. For kids who are "iffy" on new activities, it's worth looking for opportunities to "try before you buy": Sign up for a month of karate lessons before making a longer-term commitment, or try to attend a couple of sessions as observers.

The bottom line, though, is that a child who truly doesn't want to be learning piano or playing hockey is unlikely to discover the satisfaction of achievement, a sense of self-motivation, or pleasure in learning from being forced to go through the motions.

The problem is that when adults take the initiative away from a child, it diminishes her sense of mastery as well. Remember, the goal is to raise children who believe, "I can do it if I try," not "I can do it if my parents make me!"

"sub-goals" that are challenging enough to represent a real achievement for the child, yet easy enough that they are within his ability. If your child has a low tolerance for frustration, he needs small, "just-hard-enough" goals that will gradually stretch his perseverance.

Help your child have positive encounters with failure. It's a mistake, stresses Mandel, to try to protect our children from failure completely.

"It's hard to let our kids suffer," he acknowledges, "but we need to let them make mistakes, and when they do fail, help them see failing as a way of learning. Process how they feel, help them figure out what they need to do differently next time, and urge them to try again."

This doesn't mean you should *never* buffer kids from failure. Remember, a small, reversible setback can encourage perseverance; a crushing defeat can be simply crushing. Parents and teachers can guide children towards manageable challenges.

Be a good model. Kids often think that everything comes easily to grownups. Let them see you have trouble and keep trying, whether it's with a hard crossword puzzle or a night course. Say out loud what you're going through, so they know: "Boy, I feel like this job is never going to be finished! I need to think about how I'm going to manage this."

Work with her—but not for her. When you help Sarah study her spelling words or practise her hockey shots, you encourage her to stick with the task. But if you take over, and build that model castle for her, you're teaching *yourself* perseverance, not her!

A final suggestion: If the very pace of life pushes us to expect instant gratification, maybe we can, once in a while, slow things down and help our kids experience the value of working through a process. Is there a project you'd enjoy working on together? Maybe over the holidays you can spend a day making bread from scratch, or design and make a bird-house (yes, using plain old hand tools!), or learn how to make old-fashioned dipped candles. The point is to find a situation where the time and effort spent are more than the means to an end, but enjoyable in themselves. And, at the end of the day, or a few days, it won't really matter whether your bread turns out great or mediocre, your birdhouse straight or cockeyed. You learned something interesting, and you had fun working on it together—and *that's* the real success.

LOGICAL CONSEQUENCES:
TEACHING RESPONSIBILITY

n the beginning, there was "punishment." Then, as parenting pundits searched for gentler child-rearing approaches, there were "consequences" (like "withdrawing privileges" and "time-out").

Finally, we parents were encouraged to use "logical consequences" in response to our children's misbehaviour.

But what does this technical-sounding phrase really mean? It sounds suspiciously like a modern euphemism for old-fashioned punishment.

Kathy Lynn, a Vancouver parent educator and president of Parenting Today, argues that logical consequences are, in fact, quite different from punishment.

"I like to think of logical consequences as 'giving nature a nudge,'" says Lynn. "You know, every act and decision we make has a consequence. Sometimes the consequence is positive, or neutral. Sometimes it is negative. And when children experience the consequences of their actions, they learn to be responsible for their own decisions.

"Sometimes, though, parents don't want to wait for the natural consequence—perhaps it's too dangerous or severe, or perhaps it will take so long to happen that the learning will come too late. Or maybe the natural consequence will affect someone else, and you need to protect that person."

Let's imagine, for example, that your child has a bad habit of leaving his bike on the front lawn, and he's supposed to put it in the garage. The natural consequences of leaving the bike where it is are not very satisfactory: The bike may be stolen, but you aren't willing to leave your child with no bike at all, and at seven, he can't save enough to replace it himself. The bike may rust and have a shorter life—but by then your children will probably have grown out of the bike, and it's his little

1 1

"LOGICAL" DOESN'T HAVE TO MEAN "NEGATIVE"

It's almost an occupational hazard for parents to overfocus on children's misbehaviour, and let their shining moments go unnoticed. But parents can "give nature a nudge" with a logical consequence when the child makes positive choices, too!

"My eight-year-old, Jessie, had a lovely long play with her little brother last week," remembers her mother, Janice Brant. "She was very patient and accommodating with him, and as a result I was able to take care of a back-log of work. And I almost didn't say anything—you know, there's a voice inside you saying, 'Leave well enough alone' and 'Virtue is its own reward.' But I did—I gave her a big hug and told her how helpful she had been and what a nice time her brother had had, and then I said that now I'd like to do something nice for her, and asked if she would like to make fudge with me after dinner. And she just glowed!

"I felt a little funny," muses Janice, "like I was paying her to be nice. But the reality is that when you're nice to people, they feel more like being nice to you. So what's wrong with demonstrating it?"

Not a thing. Like the old proverb says, "One good turn deserves another." And a bad turn? A bad turn deserves a logical consequence—and a chance to try again.

brother (or your bank balance) that will suffer. So you decide to help nature out with a logical consequence.

What's logical about it? "The consequence," explains Lynn, "is directly connected to the child's behaviour. It demonstrates to the child the link between his action and its results. If a child leaves his bike out and as a result doesn't get to watch TV, there is no connection there. It's an arbitrary parental ruling. But if you explain, 'We have rules about bikes, and when you choose not to follow the rules, then you lose the right to ride your bike,' that makes sense. And in this specific instance you can say something like, 'You are responsible for putting your bike away at night. I'm willing to give you one reminder. But if I have to put it away myself, it's going to stay in the garage for two days.' It's like you're giving your child a foretaste of what the eventual, real consequence would be."

Lynn points out that parents sometimes get hung up on the technicalities of logical consequences (Is it totally logical? Do I have to specify the consequence in advance? Should I have a contract with rules and consequences?), when their overall parenting goals and style are far more important.

"The real difference between consequences and punishment is the intention behind them. You are asking yourself, 'What does my child need to learn from this?' not 'How much does he need to suffer?' The goal is *learning*, not retribution."

Lynn observes that a logical consequence may not even be uncomfortable for the child. "It does not have to hurt to be an effective learning experience," she says. "Parents sometimes think, for example, that there's no value in asking a child who is 'bugging' other family members to go to her room, if she has fun playing or reading once she gets there. But that's a good thing to learn: that when you're feeling antisocial, you're better off doing something on your own for a while."

When parents are thinking about learning rather than punishment, they will also find it easier to discipline according to their children's individual needs, rather than "by the book." "There are kids who need more limits and very consistent consequences," observes Lynn. "On the other hand, if your child is usually careful about his bike, but leaves it out one night because his friend is sleeping over and he's distracted, you don't need to impose a consequence. You can do him a favour and put the bike away, because he doesn't need to learn to be responsible about his bike—he already is."

When a child has caused damage, either to property or to people, a logical consequence can provide an age-appropriate way for the child to make reparation. Did she get mad and stomp on a friend's toy? Then she'll have to contribute to its replacement. Maybe she has a toy her friend likes that she could offer, or maybe she can use her allowance to contribute a percentage of the replacement cost. Instead of a "tit for tat" punishment, she has a chance to learn an important life lesson: When you make a mistake that affects another person, it's your responsibility to make things right again, to the best of your ability.

Logical consequences are most effective in a family climate where children are often allowed to make choices for themselves and experience the results. "These kids already understand that poor decisions may lead to negative consequences," says Lynn, "so logical consequences make sense to them."

PITCHING IN AND FORKING OUT:
CHORES AND ALLOWANCE

When they were babies, you were glad to wait on them hand and foot. And toddler toys are big and pretty easy to put away. By the time kids are in school, though, most parents would like to have some help around the house from their children.

That's a reasonable expectation. According to social worker and consultant Bob Fulton, helping out benefits the child as much as the parent. "If you can get the message across that 'we need your participation, you're important, we really need your help,' that will mean a lot to the child," Fulton says.

He points to extensive research that shows the benefits to children of taking on household responsibilities. "When families are under stress, the effects on the child are much less if they feel that they are contributing in some way, helping out the best they can. This really has a powerful effect."

The child who has appropriate household chores to do—even something simple like setting the table or putting away the shoes—feels needed. He or she is a contributing part of the family. As well, Fulton adds, the child who cleans up his room or vacuums the hallway gains a sense of control over his environment.

"While he may not be able to do a lot, he learns that through his own efforts he can make things a little better. And his help may make things less stressful for the parents, too, so everyone benefits."

While the value of having children participate in household chores is easy to see, getting them to actually do it can be much harder.

Debbie McGill's oldest children, Corinna (seven) and David (five), particularly resist picking up their toys. "It always seems to end with yelling and screaming, and they both insist it isn't their mess. I end up with a headache, and the toys are still lying there."

MANAGING THE MESS

What chore do parents most wish their children would do? Pick up after themselves. What chore do kids most resist doing? You got it. The reality is, *nobody* likes this job!

- Many hands make light work. Working alongside your kids is probably the only way to get the Really Big Messes cleaned up. Faced with a room full of scattered toys, a six-year-old may feel just like the kids in *The Cat in the Hat*: "And this mess is so big, and so deep, and so tall, / We cannot pick it up. There is no way at all." Looking on the bright side, this is a good opportunity to teach them how to tackle this kind of job. Rather than whipping through the lion's share as they dawdle in the corner, assign individual tasks: "Let's see ... Judy, you put the books back on the shelves. Michael, you collect up the Lego. I'll get these dress-up clothes put away, and then we'll see what's left."

- One step at a time. Big jobs do need to be defined for children. Asking a seven-year-old to "clean your room" is probably too vague a request—and her definition of a clean room isn't likely to match yours. The job can be broken down into smaller steps (for example, put dirty clothes in the laundry hamper, put books on the shelf, put toys in the toy box) that the child can handle.

- Reduce the buildup. It might work better to reduce the number of toys available and put the rest away for another day. Some families have several quick clean-up times during the day—before lunch, before supper, and before bed, for example—so that the clutter doesn't have a chance to become overwhelming.

- A place for everything. Margaret-Ann Rowan's eight-year-old daughter, Heather, did a much better job of keeping her room tidy after her Aunt Wendy helped her reorganize the room. Adding some shelves and storage containers and lowering the closet pole to Heather's height made the task easier for her. Because Wendy involved Heather in the process, she knows where everything is supposed to go.

Sometimes, especially if your child is not in a co-operative mood, it may seem easier to just do the job yourself. But Fulton says you shouldn't. He feels that the sense of obligation is essential. "If you say, 'Oh, well, I'll do it myself,' you give the child the idea that his contribution isn't really needed," he explains. "You need to stick with your expectations."

Many parents have found that balky kids will eventually get around to a chore when they invoke "Grandma's Rule": You can have X when Y. It's only a useful strategy when you can afford to wait a while, but it's kinder to both of you than an on-the-spot power struggle. The principle is simple: Good things come to people who fulfil their responsibilities. Sooner or later, the child is going to want to watch TV, or go to the park, or have a story. Your cheerful answer? "Sure. As soon as you pick up those toys."

Debbie has found that her children *do* like to set the table and wash the dishes. Since she bought them comforters for their beds, they also find bedmaking easier and will do it with some help and encouragement.

Fulton points out that making the chores appropriate and reasonable for the child's age and abilities is important. "When we got a guinea pig, it was agreed that my kids would clean out the cage once a week," recalls René Lavoie ruefully. "But they couldn't. It was a much more difficult and dirty job than we had realized—an adult job. The kids simply can't manage it without getting sodden cedar chips all over the place. So they *feed* the guinea pig, and I clean the cage."

Keeping chore time companionable helps, too. Washing dishes or folding laundry with mom or dad is much more fun than doing it alone. Many families have a "working together" time—Saturday mornings are popular—when they all contribute to cleaning up and then reward themselves with a special lunch or outing.

Some families find it works well to give kids a choice of chores. "We have a list of chores that are appropriate for kids to do, and the kids pick from the list," says Helena Maki, mother of three. "Every month or so we check whether anyone wants to change chores, and if so, we switch them around. It's been surprising to me what they choose. Mopping the kitchen floor and doing laundry are most popular, even though I thought they would be too difficult for my eight-year-old."

Helena's two younger kids each have two chores a week—they may be small daily chores like taking out the recycling, or a larger weekly chore—while her older son (age 12) does three. "But he also gets a bigger allowance," notes Helena.

Which raises yet another issue parents struggle with: Should chores be paid for, or tied to allowance in some way?

It seems a simple enough question, but there are as many answers as there are families. Most parents readily agree that children need to learn to handle money, but there is less agreement on how this lesson is best taught. Some families completely separate spending money from family chores, while others feel that children should be paid for the work they do.

Susan Cameron, for instance, believes that it is important for the children, as members of the family, to have a share of the family money, and doesn't believe it should be a reward for working. "I consider the chores they do quite separate from their allowances. If they didn't do any of their chores one week there would be another consequence—but they would still get their allowances."

The Rosten family, on the other hand, doesn't give allowances. Shelley Rosten says: "Andy and I have to earn any money we get, so we think our children should, too." Seven-year-old Jacob and older brother Ben earn their spending money by asking Mom or Dad for chores to do—anything from washing the car to washing the dishes. They are also expected to keep their rooms tidy, without payment. "I think it's important that the boys understand the connection between money and work," explains Shelley.

The Bonnici family takes a different approach. They give each of their four children an allowance—just for being part of the family. The children

SAVINGS PLANS FOR KIDS

Once children are receiving an allowance or earning spending money, the issue of saving arises.

Many Canadian banks have special programs and accounts geared to children. Briar Emond, assistant manager of personal banking with the Royal Bank of Canada, describes the Leo account they offer to children under 12.

"The Leo the Lion accounts have no service charges and no minimum balance—and we will put in $5 when the account is opened," Emond says. "The child gets a special bank book with Leo on the cover, and we also have an activity booklet called *How to Manage Your Money* for parents to go through with their children."

The Leo account is purely a savings account, and cheques can't be written on it. If parents have a Royal Bank account, though, they can arrange for a bank card for the child to use to deposit or withdraw money from a banking machine.

Many other banks have similar programs or accounts. Emond also notes that banks often send speakers to schools to talk to children about money management.

also have daily chores (like loading the dishwasher or setting the table) that aren't linked to any payment. But the family also has a list of extra "paid-for" chores that the children can take on to earn extra money.

Once children have an "income," however small, should parents exert any control over its use? Family systems run the gamut, from giving kids complete ownership over their own money to fairly rigid systems that stipulate a percentage to go into savings and to charity. It's not much of an issue with a six-year-old who only gets enough money each week to buy herself a treat at the corner store, but as kids get older parents may well want to consider ways to encourage their children to save part of their allowance for larger items.

How your family approaches the interrelated questions of how much children should contribute to the household, and whether they should be paid or receive an allowance, will depend on your own values, financial situation, and time restraints. But however you organize this aspect of family life, do keep in mind that some opportunity to learn household skills, and to manage his own money, will benefit your child. And one day (when he's big enough to cook a meal, paint a fence, or buy his own guitar), it will benefit you, too!

AT THE BARGAINING TABLE:
NEGOTIATING WITH KIDS

hy should I go to bed if I'm not tired? I should be able to stay up as late as I want!" "But I really want a pet mouse! And anyway, I can buy it myself—I have the $3 right here! All you have to pay for is the cage and food and stuff!" "I'm *not* washing my hair! It's fine the way it is."

As offers to negotiate, these opening gambits are pretty crude. Many parents would be inclined to nip them right in the bud with a firm "No," and certainly, the "Parental No" has its place. But as children get older, we are also wise to allow—even encourage—creative negotiation as a way of resolving conflicts between family members.

"In my family," recalls Flesherton, Ontario, artist Carol Wood, "my parents were like the umpire in the baseball game. A strike was a strike and you were out no matter what. It didn't matter if the video replay showed you were really safe, there was no arguing with the ump. It was so frustrating!"

With her seven-year-old daughter, Zoë, Carol has tried to be more flexible. "If we want to encourage co-operation and fair play, we need to do our bit as parents. It's not fair if kids don't have any say, and they *know* that. And even though negotiation is time-consuming, it pays off: I think that the more Zoë feels she's been a part of a decision, the more she's willing to live with it."

Therapist Stanley Shapiro is the director of the Parenting Education Centre of Ontario and co-author of *Parenting Is Not Natural* (Northwest Publishing, 1994). He promotes regular family meetings as a forum where family rules and conflicts can be worked out together. "Children and adults are all partners in the family," he says. "So children need to be included in decision-making that affects them."

Shapiro agrees with Carol Wood that negotiating with children can

2 1

STEPS TO A NEGOTIATED SETTLEMENT
Stanley Shapiro, director of the Parenting Education Centre of Ontario, suggests the following framework for resolving conflicts or solving problems within the family. Of course, you'll need to simplify the process for younger kids, but they can handle the basic scheme: State the problem, think up possible solutions, find one you both agree to.

- Start with a statement of the problem that everyone agrees to.
- Brainstorm solutions. Encourage everyone's input, and write down all ideas without criticizing.
- Pull out the ideas that everyone agrees might have some merit. Try not to get sidetracked into arguments about the ideas that aren't picked.
- Start working through details of how these ideas could be put into action: who, when, where, how. You might select just one idea or combine a few.
- Write up the solution and post it on the bulletin board or fridge.
- Set a time to sit down together and evaluate how your solution is working. If it's not working, you may need to fine-tune it or go back to brainstorming.

lead to better co-operation: "When human beings—kids or adults—are controlled or dominated, they will fight that in different ways. Kids might fight back by forgetting, arguing about, or just ignoring the rules. But if they've agreed to a rule from the beginning, they have less need to challenge it."

Carol is quick to point out that she doesn't open everything to negotiation: "Issues of health and safety—like seat belts—aren't negotiable. Or violence: Zoë is not allowed to hit her little brother Keegan, for example, and that's final. I have pretty firm rules about nutrition and TV, but everyone draws their line in a different place."

How do we negotiate with our children? First, let's clarify what we're aiming for. Adversarial negotiations—in which each participant tries to win, with little regard for the other's interests—are *not* likely to promote family harmony. We're talking about negotiation as a co-operative problem-solving process that seeks a "win-win" solution: a solution that meets everyone's needs and that everyone involved can agree to.

Here's how Carol and her daughter worked through Zoë's birthday party plans. "I hate birthday parties," says Carol frankly, "and I've come to dread them because Zoë always gets 'birthday girl meltdown'—crying when someone pops a balloon, or about anything else that's not quite perfect, and becoming very needy of my attention. So I sat her down this year and laid it on the line. I just explained why I find parties so stressful, and said, "I know you want to feel special on your birthday, but during the party, we're both the hostesses and I need you to be on my team, helping the other kids have a nice time."

Wood also offered her daughter other options: having a couple of friends over, or having a long "special" day with just family, but Zoë was insistent on the big group. "So we listed the things I needed for her to do, and she agreed to them and to the condition that if the party didn't work out this year, we wouldn't have one next year." Wood had some concerns about the agreement. "This was hard for her, and she had a lot at stake." But Zoë came through, and she and her mother both count the party a success.

Negotiation is a learning process for both parents and kids, and it will evolve from offering simple choices to a toddler to grappling with complex, difficult issues with your teen. Some tips to guide your progress:

Be clear about what you're willing to open for negotiation. If you've already decided on a firm bedtime, then it's frustrating and unfair to initiate a discussion about "what bedtime should be." However, including children in decisions about how the bedtime routine is handled is definitely still worthwhile.

People are sometimes leery about negotiating with kids because they fear constant harassment from children who believe that, as Carol puts it, "No never really means no." She is very clear with Zoë about issues where final decision-making power rests with the parent: "I'll consider your arguments carefully, but whatever my answer is, it's final."

Of course we all make errors in judgement, and it's important to be willing to admit them. "Zoë put on her gymnastics suit to wear to school the other day," recalls Carol, "and my first reaction was, 'You're not going out the door in that.' She asked, 'Why not?' And I couldn't think of one good reason." Carol's advice for avoiding long-drawn-out arguments is simple: "If you're prepared to capitulate, do it fast!"

A child who can negotiate fairly and problem-solve creatively is heading into life with an incredibly useful interpersonal skill. You're raising a kid who will be able to ask for a raise, divide up housework with a roommate, and work through conflicts with a future partner. He's learning that he can stand up for his own interests, while still respecting other people's; that people who disagree can still help each other and work together. We may joke about the waist-high "junior lawyers" in our lives—but look ahead to the future. These kids are going to be awesome.

"NO FAIR!" JUSTICE, SIBLING-STYLE

 t started not over ice cream but over the ice cream bowls. Seven-year-old Jerod had finished his dinner first and asked for dessert. His six-year-old sister, Ariel, still working on her meal, eyed him resentfully.

"It's not fair!" she said. "Jerod got the new bowl!" When Ariel got her serving, there was a new complaint: "Jerod got more than me!" (Their mother, Kim Elliott, swears they both had exactly the same amount.)

"It's not fair!" Parents can count on hearing those words many times over as their children grow, no matter how hard they try to treat their children equally. In fact, according to Lynda Lougheed of Information Children in Vancouver, it's possible to go too far in trying to be fair and end up causing even more rivalry.

"The truth is, things aren't always fair," she explains. "Of course, we want to be fair within reason—obvious favouritism towards one child would be very hurtful. But rather than trying to treat all our children exactly the same, it's better to treat each one as special and unique."

If, for example, you try to avoid the "No fair!" comments by buying two (or three, or four) of everything, you run the risk of missing the individual needs of each child. It's like deciding that since your first baby needed to nurse every two hours, you'll feed your second baby every two hours as well. That might be too often—or not often enough.

If Jenny has outgrown her winter coat this year, but Jacob's still fits fine and is in good condition, do you buy them both new coats? Or do you focus on the needs of the individual—Jenny needs a new coat and Jacob doesn't? (He might need boots, though.) Similar issues come up on birthdays—do you buy the non-birthday child a gift, too, so that he or she won't feel left out? Lougheed feels that the "everyone gets the

"MOM ALWAYS LIKED YOU BEST!" *Facing Up to Favouritism*
We all want to love our children equally, but the reality is that some children (or different children, at different ages) may be "easier" to love than others. Maybe you have a good personality fit and shared interests with your quiet, studious daughter, while your exuberant, active son gets on your nerves. Maybe your even-tempered, accommodating middle-schooler is nicer to be with these days than your moody, mouthy adolescent. What can you do?

First of all, suggests Nancy Samalin, accept that it's normal to connect more easily with one child than another. "There's nothing wrong with *feeling* this way," she says. "The danger is when we *act* on our feelings."

Every child needs a positive relationship with her parents. Sometimes it takes more of an effort to build that strong connection with a child, but the rewards for both of you are well worth it. Look for ways to appreciate, understand, and enjoy your more challenging child. What do you enjoy doing together? What qualities or actions can you admire in him? How can you let her know, with actions as well as words, that you love her deeply even when you're having trouble getting along together?

same" approach actually encourages the children to focus on comparing rather than on what they need.

Kim Elliott tries to respond to her children as individuals, so she answered Ariel's outburst by helping her express her needs. "I told her that she should ask me for what she wants instead of complaining about what Jerod has."

For example, when Ariel complained about Jerod getting a new bowl, Kim asked her, "Do you want a new bowl, too?" When she complained that he had more ice cream, Kim suggested: "If you're still hungry when you're finished yours, you can ask me for some more." There were a few tears, but Ariel was able to tell her mother what she wanted—a new bowl and a little bit more ice cream.

Other "fairness" issues may require some negotiations. Children between the ages of six and eight are developing a very strong awareness of rules, and this provides a good opportunity to let them work out their problems. "Parents tend to step in and solve kids' problems," Lougheed points out. "But if you always do that, they don't get a chance to develop their problem-solving skills. Instead of telling them what to do, encourage them to come up with their own solutions—and they'll create something that seems fair to them."

Kim's children fought over who would get to sit in the front of the car during outings, for example. But when she insisted that they find a solution to this ongoing problem, they quickly decided that one would sit in the front on the way out, and the other on the way home. They both feel that's fair, and there's no more arguing. (This gets more complicated, of course, when you have three, four, or more children!)

However, even careful negotiation and planning won't eliminate all complaints of unfairness, and the battles can be tough for parents to handle. Kim observes: "Young children can't learn this in a single day. You have to expect to hear 'no fair' over and over until they work through how to ask for things in a better way, or how to solve a problem with another child."

> **RECOMMENDED READING**
>
> *Loving Each One Best: A Caring and Practical Approach to Raising Siblings*, by Nancy Samalin, Bantam Books, 1996.

Lougheed adds, "When we've surveyed parents and asked them what they like least about parenting, we always get one answer far more often than any other: 'sibling rivalry.' And that's what those complaints of 'no fair' are, most often."

To reduce this kind of rivalry, keep the focus on the uniqueness of each child. Don't make comparisons, and if one child complains "It's not fair!" try to uncover the underlying need that's being expressed. Is she hungry, feeling a bit ignored, or just in need of some reassurance that she's still loved and important to you? Rather than arguing whether Joni did or did not get more new clothes or more hugs, bring the conversation back to your child's individual case: "I guess you sometimes get tired of wearing your sister's hand-me-downs," or "Do you need some cuddle time? C'mon on my lap here and let me give you a big bear hug!"

In her book, *Loving Each One Best*, parent educator Nancy Samalin sums it up beautifully:

> *When a child complains, "It's not fair!" ... you can listen and respond to the deeper cry, which is: "Do you hear me? Do you see me as an individual? Am I separate, special, respected, interesting, enjoyable, lovable? Do you appreciate me for who I am?" Then, instead of counting the marshmallows in the hot chocolate, you can try to respond to the message behind the words.*

"KEEP OUT!" THE NEED FOR PRIVACY

EEP OWT! THIS MEENS YOU. The hand-lettered sign stuck to the firmly closed bedroom door is a shock, coming as it does from a child who only last year wanted "company" to go upstairs to the bathroom. But if the spelling is a little shaky, the intent is clear: This is a declaration of private territory.

Your first inclination may be to walk in, anyway. "I'm your *mother*, for heaven's sake. I've slept with my bedroom door open for years so I can hear you if you wake up. And now you tell me to *keep out?!*"

But on second thought, most of us will recognize this sign as a signal of growth, and knock first. Teri Degler, author of the parenting guide *Love, Limits, and Consequences* (Summerhill Press, 1990) and former education specialist with emotionally disturbed children, notes that the emerging need for privacy is part of a child's developing independence. "The desire for private space often surfaces around age six or seven," she observes. "You see it in the classic sign on the door, the box with a lock for 'secret treasures,' even a first diary for kids who like writing."

If a sudden renewed intensity about his possessions ("Don't even *touch* my hockey cards—they're mine!") reminds you of his toddler days, a new tendency to spend time alone in his room listening to the radio may seem disconcertingly adolescent. The comparison is quite apt. Says Degler, "Kids develop in a cyclical pattern—the same issues emerge repeatedly. They take a leap forward—'I can do everything myself'—and then run back to you. I think the stages we see of wanting privacy and their own space correspond to times when they're stepping away from you, moving towards more independence. And that, after all, is the whole point of childhood: gradually learning to be an independent adult."

Unfortunately, at this age kids' need for privacy isn't always balanced by corresponding good judgement or reliability. That makes for a difficult judgement call for parents: You don't want to barge in on Tyler in the bath when he wants to be alone, but you just know the soap will remain untouched if you don't.

Degler notes that children mature at very different rates, and that age alone doesn't tell us how much freedom a child can handle. It comes down to knowing your own child. "You give increasing amounts of privacy, based on children's demonstrated ability to handle responsibility and to do what they say they are going to do. You can say to them: 'I want to give you this privacy. Let's start with a little bit, and you show me you can handle it.'"

Inevitably there will be "mistakes." When Jane Morton's seven-year-old son went to play in the basement with a friend, amidst great fanfare and secrecy ("Nobody come down here! We're working on a special project!"), she thought little about it. "They'd played down there before, making clubhouses out of boxes, bringing in comics and stuff. But when I went down to do laundry after dinner, I discovered a huge mess and a row of glass jars filled with terrible-looking fluids. Ben called it a 'lab' and the jars 'potions'—and eventually admitted that not only had they snuck stuff from the kitchen and laundry for potion ingredients, they had gone into the tool room (absolutely forbidden) and helped themselves to things like pruning paint and WD-40!"

The action Jane took fits well with Teri Degler's advice: "First, if damage has been done, there should be whatever the normal consequences would be to repair the damage." In this case, Ben and his friend had a large clean-up job to do, after Jane had disposed of the 'potions.' "Second," says Degler, "you probably need to take a step backwards in the amount of privacy or freedom the child is allowed: 'What this shows me is that you can't handle as much freedom as we thought. For now, you're going to have to be supervised more closely.'" Jane told Ben that he would not be playing alone in the basement for some time. She also pointed out that she would be able to respect his desire for privacy with

---

"STOP LOOKING AT ME!" *Siblings and Privacy*
Siblings often have intense conflicts over privacy matters, especially when one is just too young to understand the desire to be alone. "Why won't she let me watch her play Pound Puppies?" sobs your four-year-old—and while you do understand the new self-consciousness that cramps your daughter's pretend play when an audience is present, you ache, as well, for the rejected little brother. Some families declare that play requiring privacy belongs in a private room (i.e., no kicking little brothers out of the family room!)—which works just fine, as long as the kids each *have* a private room.

Sharing a room becomes a special challenge at this age; many of us will remember drawing imaginary lines between the beds, as well as the taunts and skirmishes that ensued. Parents can help by finding their school-age child some "inviolable" space for her most private things—perhaps a shelf too high for prying younger siblings, or a box with a lock and key. And parents might be ready to lend their own room now and then, when a private play space is needed.

Finally, if open bath- and bedroom doors have been the norm in your home, be prepared to support the child who starts closing them. Again, tactful explanations to younger siblings may be required: "Mike's getting older now, and he wants to be alone in the bathroom. When he closes the door, that means we don't go in until he's finished."

---

his friends when he had shown her that he could respect their rules about safety and using other people's things—even when she wasn't there to remind him.

Your child needs some private "inner space" now, too. You may realize that she doesn't necessarily *want to* tell you "everything" any more. You can't force her to tell you her problems, but you can develop the skill of inviting confidences. "Kids need to know they can tell us the bad as well as the good," says Degler. "If they've come to expect a fair hearing, not an automatic blow-up, they'll be more willing to come to us for help."

"I hear Ben talking to himself in bed sometimes before he goes to sleep," says Jane. "I can't quite make out what he's saying, but it's clearly some sort of storyline, complete with dialogue and sound effects. If I come in to say goodnight or put something away, he stops dead.

"It's so tempting to eavesdrop," she admits. "It's really cute, what he's doing. But I know I can't. This is his own private fantasy, and I have to respect that."

BEYOND BIRDS AND BEES: TALKING ABOUT SEX

hy were the big kids laughing when Spot got on that other dog?" "Drew and I were playing doctor. He said I should kiss his dinky to make it better. Is that okay?" "I understand how babies come out of the Mommy—but how do they get in?"

Perhaps you've already had to respond to one or all of the above childhood queries. If you were able to do so without blushing, stammering, or audibly gasping for air at least once, give yourself full marks.

Most of us, though, aren't quite as matter-of-fact about "sex questions" as we might like to be. We want to raise sexually healthy children, but aren't sure how! We're the ones who have hang-ups dating back to our own childhoods, or who are afraid of telling our kids too much too soon. Maybe our answers will lead to premature experimentation. Or maybe we're afraid of giving out the wrong information (some of the simplest questions seem to require the most complex, scientific answers!), or we can't decide whether to pass along our sexual knowledge using the slang terms of the street or the anatomically correct words that will help earn them As in biology later on. Why do young children ask so darned many questions about sex anyway? Couldn't this ordeal be postponed till closer to the kids' high school graduation?

The answer is *no*. For as author Lynn Leight so clearly notes in her book *Raising Sexually Healthy Children*, we are living in an era of AIDS and escalating reports of child sexual abuse, which have "legitimized a child's right to know." It's no longer a matter of "Can we talk?" but rather "We must talk." In Leight's words: "Honest communication about sexuality is necessary to preserve the health, welfare, and personal happiness of your child."

Clearly, it's no longer sufficient (if indeed it ever was) to wait until

BOOKS AND VIDEOS FOR PARENTS AND KIDS TO SHARE
Questions Children Ask & How to Answer Them, by Dr. Miriam Stoppard, Random House, 1997. Stoppard gives examples of the kinds of questions kids ask and worry about, including a section on sex and birth, and gives sample answers appropriate for different age groups.

Speaking of Sex: Are You Ready to Answer the Questions Your Kids Will Ask? by Meg Hickling, RN, Northstone, 1996. A frank, sensible, compassionate, and even funny book, full of real-life questions and answers.

Where Did I Come From? Rocket Pictures Home Video, distributed by Coscient Astral. This animated video narrated by Howie Mandel covers all aspects of human reproduction quite frankly, but with a light-hearted, natural tone.

your child reaches puberty before offering a cloudy explanation of sex in terms of "the birds and the bees." Explaining where babies come from is part of your child's sex education—but there is much, much more!

This is because sex is more than what happens when penis and vagina meet. It involves moral values, self-esteem, making responsible decisions. Kids need to know not just how things happen, but why. They need reassurance that the physical and emotional changes they experience as they grow older are normal and healthy.

Almost every contemporary sex education book on the market strongly urges parents to become the primary sex educators for their children. Children who receive direct, factual, non-threatening answers to their questions about sexuality keep going back to their parents regarding sexual values and information. Consider: To whom might they turn for answers in your place? This could well provide the jolt you need to brush up on your sexuality responses!

"Help them understand that, as a family, you can discuss any subject openly and without embarrassment," advise the authors of *The Caring Parent's Guide: Sexuality Education at Home*. It's also considered prudent to "temper the facts with your values... let your children know what you believe and what you expect of them. See to it that they

WHAT SHOULD THEY KNOW?

Meg Hickling, a BC sex educator and author of *Speaking of Sex*, does believe in giving children information early, and some parents may be more comfortable with a somewhat slower learning curve. That said, Hickling suggests that by the end of the primary grades, children need to know:

- the names for genitals: penis, testicles, vulva, vagina, etc.
- "scientific" names having to do with excretion: urine, bladder, anus, etc.
- the distinction between the digestive and reproductive systems
- that reproduction happens when a man's sperm joins a woman's ovum by sexual intercourse, and what sexual intercourse is
- that the baby grows in the uterus and is born through the vagina
- fairly complete information about menses and nocturnal emissions (some girls do start menstruating as early as age eight)
- introductory information about puberty
- not to pick up old condoms

Unfortunately, our kids also need some knowledge about the sexual abuse of children. "Care for Kids," a broad-based early-childhood sexual-education and abuse-prevention program, suggests the following key messages:

- Adults and older children have no business "playing" with a child's private parts (or genitals). Sometimes adults need to help children with washing or wiping their private parts, but that's not the same as playing with them.
- Adults and older children do not need help with their private parts. If for some reason they do, they should ask another adult, not a child.
- It's OK to say no to any kind of touching that makes you uncomfortable.
- Touching is never a secret.
- When we are feeling "mixed up" or upset about anything (including touching, secrets, feelings, or private parts), we can ask adults for help.

Above all, show your child that she can confide in you by your willingness to answer her questions about sex and anatomy. It is very hard for most children to tell someone that they have been abused. In a family where the whole topic of sex is avoided, it will be that much harder.

understand the responsibilities that go hand-in-hand with sexuality."

It all may seem a bit much for an innocent little six-year-old but remember, you don't have to do the whole thing at once. Frequent, short conversations that take advantage of a "teachable moment" are much more suited to a young child's learning style, anyway.

Some parents may be tempted to focus in on just the "essential information" needed to help protect children from sexual-abuse, but is this really a healthy approach? Denise Gaulin, a sexual-health educator and public-health nurse with the Leeds, Grenville, and Lanark (Ontario) District Health Unit, and one of the creators of the Care for Kids early-childhood sexuality-education program, doesn't think so: "I feel strongly that the first messages that children hear about sexuality should not be in the context of abuse," says Gaulin. "Do we really want our children to be introduced to the sick side before they are introduced to the nice side?" Care for Kids, developed by an interdisciplinary team to address child abuse issues within their region, instead educates children about abuse within the broader context of healthy and developmentally appropriate messages about sexuality.

Community libraries offer an abundance of literature—much of it written and illustrated in a way that makes it fun for parent and child to review together. The use of cartoons serves as a kind of "icebreaker" for many parents who aren't yet ready to handle anything too graphic. *A Kid's First Book about Sex*, written by Joani Blank and illustrated by Marcia Quackenbush, is a good example of this.

We all need to keep our parental eyes and ears open for what Leight calls those "golden opportunities" to foster healthy attitudes about sexuality. That means treating children's curiosity about anatomy and other sex-related issues as a normal, healthy part of development, and helping them feel good about this aspect of their identity, not guilty or ashamed. It means answering questions to the best of your ability, drawing on books, videos, and other resources when appropriate. Sex becomes a "dirty" word only when it's treated as a taboo subject.

OUT OF THE NEST
Your Child in the World

Brenda Cooke

REMEMBER THE DAYS WHEN YOU WERE the unquestioned authority on almost everything? You've probably noticed that those days have slipped away—and now your statements may be contradicted with, "But Mr. Miller says..." or "But at Jamie's house they never do that..." Your child is discovering a big world beyond your home, and learning about new possibilities and different points of view.

It's an exciting time for your child, although sometimes challenging, too. Friendships become increasingly important. This is the time when many social skills are developed: learning to work together, to argue and still stay friends, to tolerate and understand differences.

Not all children move into the wider world at the same speed. While Claire is enthusiastic about school, her soccer team, and visiting friends, her more cautious cousin Sam finds those long school days very taxing, refuses to sign up for any activities, and insists that friends come over to his house to play. So Claire's dad worries that she's overextending herself, while his sister (Sam's mom) worries that Sam is too much of a loner. When children develop in ways that are a little to the side of the beaten track, parents do tend to wonder whether they're "adjusting OK," even if they seem happy. Most often, though, kids like Claire and Sam are simply exploring their world at their own pace, and in a way that matches their own personalities. And really, would you want it any other way?

"*I CAN HANDLE IT*": ENCOURAGING INDEPENDENCE

● ●

for Kathy O'Mara, the experience was a revelation. She'd always hated the aftermath of swimming lessons, when she rushed around trying to get her son Luke and his friend Colin (both seven) dried, dressed, and out to the car. She'd dress Luke, dry and brush his hair, tie up his shoes, and then repeat the whole process with Colin. And then, one week, she noticed another mother in the change room, with four children all apparently under age six.

"She was doing better with four than I was with two!" Kathy says. She noticed that the children were all getting themselves showered, dried, and dressed—and helping their younger siblings as well. Their mother had a baby to tend to, and when the baby was ready, the mother just waited patiently until her older children had finished their tasks.

"I realized that I had a tendency to always jump in and help if my kids weren't doing things fast enough, or the way I would have done it," Kathy says. "But children have their own pace. I still struggle with that urge to rush in and take over, but at least I'm more aware of it."

Allowing children to develop independence—to do things for themselves—is a vital part of parenting, according to Linda Tetreault, a teacher in the Social Services Worker program at Sheridan College.

"We need to encourage independence in children because it helps them grow up to be stronger adults who are less likely to be victimized," she explains.

There are two aspects to independence: making choices and taking responsibility, and they are firmly linked together. Tetreault feels that making choices should begin as soon as the child is able to communicate. Some things, of course, are not negotiable, but often the child can choose (for example) whether to read in bed before going to sleep, or whether he wants a nightlight, even if he can't choose his bedtime.

SENSIBLY SAFE OR OVERPROTECTIVE? THE FINE LINE
How do you know when to allow kids to try their wings, and when to rein them in and keep them safe? The short answer is, you don't. Parenthood is full of decisions you can never be entirely sure of, and finding that magical blend of independence and protection is one of the toughest.

You can make good guesses, though, based on what you know about your child's abilities. Preparation is important, too. "Freedoms must be given gradually," says Alison Rees, a counsellor and parent educator in Victoria, BC. "You can't just say one day, 'OK, you're ten now, you can ride your bike on the street by yourself.' That would be useless, if the child hasn't been prepared by riding in an empty parking lot, riding on the sidewalk, going for family bike rides where you instruct and model safe riding."

"Overprotectiveness is not allowing kids to take normal risks," says Rees. But whether that's playing on the high climber or crossing the street alone, there is no easy formula for what defines a "normal risk." In many smaller communities in Canada, for example, some children in grade one walk to school with a friend or older sibling. In our urban centres, that may be out of the question. Says Rees, "It's the parent's job to evaluate, with the child, the boundary that is being negotiated. You discuss the situation, educate the kids, and when you think they're ready, let them go."

As Kathy O'Mara points out, when a child is offered a choice, parents must be prepared to live with the decision. "Luke is very involved in sports, and when he had the opportunity to attend a special sports camp for the summer, we thought it would be great. But we felt he should be given the choice, and he decided he'd rather spend the summer just playing with his friends. We were a little disappointed, but encouraging independence, to me, means allowing him to make these decisions."

Tetreault agrees that sometimes parenting an independent child can be more difficult. "Because they have learned (through making choices) that there *are* alternatives, they may tend to sass back and question the rules—but they have higher self-esteem and they're emotionally healthier. They will learn to respect you if the message is clear that you respect them."

"CAN I HAVE A PET? I'LL LOOK AFTER HIM ..."
Is a pet a good way to teach a school-aged child about independence and responsibility?

Veterinarian Karen Smith's Nova Scotia home is full of kids and animals, and she is unequivocal about the value of a pet in a child's life. She warns, though, that a pet's well-being shouldn't depend entirely on a child: "Parents often hope that children will learn responsibility by caring for a dog or cat, but your expectations shouldn't be too high. Often the parent ends up doing most of the work, so it's important that the pet you choose fit into your lifestyle."

Children can certainly be involved in their pet's care, but even small, "low-maintenance" pets usually require an adult's active help. Your seven-year-old, for example, can feed his fish every day (with occasional reminding), but if you think he's going to be in charge of cleaning out the tank, you might want to get a demo from a friend who keeps fish before committing yourself (I still remember dropping a tank that was just too heavy and awkward for me to manage safely at the age of ten).

Similarly, your eight-year-old may be able to walk a dog—but only after the pet is perfectly trained, so you know he won't take off after a squirrel and drag your child onto the road. And even then, only an adult or older child can safely provide the really long rambles most young, active dogs need.

So, if you and your child like animals, by all means get him a pet. As Smith says, "A pet is a friend who is non-judgemental, who always loves you, who doesn't get upset about his job or the economy. You can play with your pet, let him sleep on your bed, talk to him when nobody else wants to hear your problems ... and he won't talk back."

But the bottom line is that with a pet—even a little, inexpensive pet—you take on responsibility for that animal's life. That's a responsibility that young kids can share, but it's usually too much for them to handle alone.

Gail Southwick is the mother of eleven-year-old Kimberley, eight-year-old Adam, and six-year-old twins Daniel and Sarah. She tries to "teach independence through responsibility."

Gail uses the normal events in the children's lives to introduce new responsibilities. For example, at the beginning of each summer they go over the "rules of the summer." This year, Adam was allowed for the first time to go to the nearby playground alone and to go around the block on his bike.

Learning to make choices, and accepting the responsibility for these choices, is a very important skill, Gail feels. "When they're little, you tend to arrange everything for them, but as they go out into the world, you have to rely on them to make good decisions on their own. If they've learned at home to express themselves and think about what could happen, then they'll make good choices as they go along."

Gail comments that the innate drive for independence seems much stronger in some children than others. "I notice it most clearly in my twins, because one is very dependent and the other quite independent, even though they're both the same age. Daniel needs to take small steps to try new things, he tends to be hesitant, while Sarah tries to hurry him along."

These individual differences need to be taken into account as you help your child move towards greater independence. Choices and responsibilities should always be both age-appropriate and appropriate for the individual child.

Helping your children become more independent is most often a matter of simply stepping back a little and allowing them to move into the wider world at their own speed. "It's hard sometimes," says Tetreault, "but it's worth it."

STARTING GRADE ONE: THE
TRANSITION TO FULL-TIME SCHOOL

nce upon a time, starting grade one was like entering another world. For many children, this was a huge transition, marking their first time away from home or with a large group of kids and certainly their first time inside a school. The structure and demands of the classroom, too, were entirely new.

Today, most children get a more gradual introduction to school in the form of kindergarten. Odds are, they enter grade one familiar with the school building, comfortable with the daily separation from their family, and knowing at least a few kids in their class. And, in most schools, the grade-one classroom is a more child-friendly environment designed to "ease" children from kindergarten's play-based program to a more academic focus.

"When Paige started kindergarten she used to come home exhausted," recalls Cynthia Hickey, whose daughter started grade one last year. "So I thought that staying the whole day would really wipe her out at first. But she seemed to know how to pace herself, and she adapted quite easily."

Many children, like Paige, thrive in grade one from the start. But for others, it's important to remember that "big school" is still a big step. Many first-graders—even when they enjoy school—come home tired, stressed, and hard to get along with after a full day in the classroom.

Kathy Cunningham was taken aback by how grumpy and argumentative her six-year-old daughter, Kylie, was at the end of the day. When Kathy talked to some other mothers, though, she discovered Kylie was far from unique.

Annette Caine, a teacher at the Froebel School in Mississauga, Ontario, sees how difficult it is for some children to make the adjustment to attending school for a full day. "Some of them are just stretched

THE STRESSES OF SCHOOL CULTURE

Some of the most challenging changes facing the grade one student may not have anything to do with the actual classroom program. Consider these examples, all drawn from real life:

- Shortly after beginning school, Maya started dragging her heels every morning. It took her parents a while to discover that everything was fine at school—it was the big, noisy bus ride Maya hated. "I never know where to sit, and sometimes the bus starts going before I find a place and I almost fall. I hate having to sit with big kids I don't even know," she blurted out one day.

- Jason was always ravenous when he got home—yet his lunch was largely uneaten. When first asked about it, he just shrugged. But in the weeks that followed, he gradually described an array of problems: He had trouble getting the top off the yogurt, and once when he pulled hard it splattered out on his shirt. His carrots were "yucky" after sitting in a warm desk all morning. And anyway, the children only had ten minutes to eat before being shooed into the playground. If he and his friends got laughing and talking, he just didn't have time to eat.

- "What do you do at recess?" Kim's father asked one evening. "Oh, mostly we just stand against the wall," answered Kim. "The big kids are always using everything."

to their limit by late afternoon. They're winding down. At the same time, their ability to interact with each other deteriorates pretty quickly. They easily become frustrated and often cry if something goes wrong." These kids are often still trying hard to live up to the rules and other expectations in the classroom. "Once they get home, they just let it all out—they can't hold it in any longer," says Caine.

Janie Jolley, a grade one/two teacher at John Muir Elementary School in Sooke district, BC, has some suggestions to help children adjust to full-time school:

To a certain extent, the big, noisy world of the schoolyard just takes getting used to. But there are ways parents can help:

- Lunchtime is worth some attention, because a hungry child is going to have a harder time coping. If your child will be taking her lunch, have a few "lunchbag picnics" before school starts to check her abilities. Can she manage the lids of those plastic containers you're planning to use? Does she know how to pack up the leftovers so her lunchbox doesn't end up awash in grape juice or pudding? Once school starts, ask her sometimes how she liked her lunch. It's amazing how many foods that are accepted at home quietly end up in the garbage at school (too messy, too smelly, too time-consuming...).
- If your child is easily intimidated by a group, you might talk with the teacher about buddying him up with another child. "I will often make sure a child like this has someone to go out to the playground with," says grade one/two teacher Janie Jolley.
- Ditto for the bus. If there's no obvious "buddy" for your child, you might talk to the bus driver about saving the first few rows of seats for the youngest children to use.

Cut them some slack. Try not to schedule other new things during the first few months of school. "Suddenly, they are in school twice as long. For many children, that's about all they can cope with at first," says Jolley. "You may need to curtail activities like swimming and Sprites until around Thanksgiving."

Get organized. "Everyone is more confident when they feel on top of things," notes Jolley. "Parents can help by keeping track of library days, forms that need returning, gym clothes, and so on."

Feed them. Hunger often seems to be a factor when children are feeling miserable. Try sending along a nutritious snack for afternoon recess, and have a snack ready and waiting when they walk in the door.

Give them "re-entry" time. Some kids need to "veg out" for a while after school—don't expect young students to play nicely with younger siblings or go outside right away. This might be a good time for a favourite video or to listen to a story read aloud. Some children, however, especially if their classroom routine has required a lot of "sitting still," will want to head outside and work off their excess energy.

Keep in touch with your child. It's hard to offer effective support if you don't know what's going on. Yet it can take some creativity to get beyond "school's OK." Jolley suggests that specific questions like "What story did the teacher read in library today?" can be fruitful. "Kids aren't necessarily going to just walk in the door and start talking," says Cynthia Hickey. "When Paige gets home, we empty her backpack together and look at her work and any notes. That helps her remember what happened that day."

Kathy Cunningham's solution was to volunteer as a lunch monitor at Kylie's school. The teachers didn't mind her bringing Kylie's younger siblings, and that middle-of-the-day contact with her family helped Kylie handle being at school the rest of the time. Although Kathy's duties kept her busy, Kylie always welcomed her eagerly and chatted happily with her sisters. "I'd really recommend becoming involved in your child's classroom if you can. It seems to help Kylie a lot just to see me every day, to know I'll be dropping in," says Kathy.

RECOMMENDED READING

Here's a book that you'll dip into year after year, to help you work with your child's teacher and school to support his learning:

The School Solution: Getting Canada's Schools to Work for Your Children, by Paul Kropp and Lynda Hodson, Random House, 1995.

Keep in touch with the teacher. Teachers welcome parents' questions about how a child's school experience is going, and need to be aware of school-related problems you may have at home. Annette Caine suggests that if your child is taking much longer than two or three months to "settle in" to his class, or if he seems very tired or unhappy about school, you should talk with the teacher. "Often it's the parents who see the first signs of stress," agrees Jolley. "A child might seem to be doing fine at school, but fall apart when he gets home." Jolley notes that teachers also appreciate hearing about other difficult (or happy) experiences in a child's life. "When a child is under a lot of stress, he's not available for learning," says Jolley. "If we know that, we can ease up at school, and focus more on supporting the child."

While grade one brings plenty of academic challenges, Jolley's November interview tends to focus first on the child's overall adjustment. "You have to look at, is she liking school? Is she comfortable here? When that falls into place, then a child is ready to focus on learning."

FRIENDS, INDEED! THE SOCIAL WHIRL BEGINS

What is a friend? That depends, partly, on how old you are. In the early school years, children's friendships grow in complexity and importance.

As father of two, John Sinclair observes, "With preschoolers, friendship seems almost to be a matter of convenience: Your friend is whoever is handy, the kid next door or who sits beside you at snacktime—or the one with the best toys at his house."

He's noticed a change in his seven-year-old, Thomas, though: "Thomas's friendships seem to be based now on personality: He wants to be with kids who share his interests and who he can get along with easily—kids he likes."

That's a key element in the evolution of friendships in this age group, agrees Janet Morrison, a child psychotherapist in Toronto. "These kids have moved beyond parallel play. When they're with a friend, they want to be interacting with that friend. It's a more intense involvement, so compatibility of personality, interests, and activity level all become important."

"There's a boy Thomas has been friends with for years," says Sinclair. "They've always hung out together a lot. But now Thomas is realizing that they don't really like to do the same things. They don't have that much in common."

In fact, a strong theme with friendships in these years has to do with finding common ground and differences. "Now kids want to be like their friends. They're starting to want the same clothes, the same toys, to watch the same TV shows," notes Morrison. "At the same time, they're noticing differences. First, the differences between their family and other families, as they spend more time in their friends' homes. But

---

BEST FRIEND BLUES

Seven-year-old Drew had two best friends: Simon and Tyler. But he also had a problem: Simon didn't like Tyler. In fact, Simon teased Tyler at school and tried to persuade the other kids not to speak to him.

"It was really bothering Drew," recalls his mother, Lynn Banting. "He couldn't understand why Simon was being mean to Tyler, and he really wanted to play with both of them."

Drew talked his problem over with his parents, but he came up with his own plan. "He decided to invite them both for a sleepover party, to help them become friends. This was their first sleepover, so it was a really big deal," smiles Lynn. "We did a lot of planning to make sure it was going to be so fun they would both want to come."

Drew's strategy worked beautifully. "They spent so much time talking about and planning the sleepover, that by the time the day arrived Simon and Tyler were already getting along much better. Tyler didn't actually stay overnight—his parents didn't think he was quite ready for a sleepover—but he stayed pretty late and the boys had a great time together."

"I really admired how Drew handled this," adds Lynn. "He didn't just accept the situation, or side with one kid against the other. He thought hard about how to help both friends make peace. And he realized that his plan might not work—he was thinking about what else he might try if it didn't."

Being torn between two friends is a difficult and all too common dilemma for kids. Sometimes one friend is possessive, and tries to drive away any potential competitors. Sometimes it's just one of those inexplicable enmities. And it's not always possible to mend fences as successfully as Drew did. But there is a truth here: When kids are having fun together, it's hard for them to dislike each other. It's definitely worth a try.

---

also differences between children—and that, unfortunately, can lead to some children being rejected."

Last year, in kindergarten, one of Heidi Pieper's best friends was a boy in her class.

STEPS & STAGES: THE EARLY SCHOOL YEARS

Not any more. Now, in grade one, seven-year-old Heidi is "not interested in him any more," says her mom, Chantal Côté-Pieper of Ile Perrôt, Québec. "He calls sometimes, but she only wants to play with girls." In fact, Heidi feels so strongly about this that she actually called the boy's mother. "I walked in the room just in time to hear her say, 'Madame, your son is being very impolite. Would you tell him to stop bothering me, please,'" recalls Chantal.

Not all kids are so self-assured in the way they handle it, but most children, says Morrison, will stick to same-sex friendships in these years. "The exception is friendships that can exist 'outside the rules,'" she notes. Opposite-sex cousins or next-door neighbours may continue to play together, away from the observant eyes of schoolmates, but on the playground segregation is the norm.

While preschoolers still have most of their emotional needs met within the family, from now on children look increasingly to their friends for approval and companionship. In his book *How to Raise a Child with a High EQ: A Parents' Guide to Emotional Intelligence*, Lawrence Shapiro writes: "Friendships among children imprint a lifetime of habits in relating to others, as well as a sense of one's own self-esteem nearly equal to that developed by parental love and nurturance. Conversely, when a child lacks friends or peer acceptance, particularly in the elementary school years, he carries with him a sense of incompleteness and unfulfillment."

That doesn't mean that children need to have a large, busy social circle. As Morrison points out, "There is a huge diversity in how gregarious people are. Some children want to spend every waking moment with their friends, while others need and enjoy a fair bit of solitude. But even a shy, quiet child will normally have one or two good friends that she enjoys spending time with. If a child has no friends at all, then something is wrong."

When this is a pervasive, long-term problem, the support of a therapist may be needed. Often, though, lack of friends is a temporary situation: a best friend moves away, leaving a painful gap, or a child starts a new school where she doesn't know anybody. While many children will easily strike up new friendships on their own, it can take time both to be accepted by a new group of kids and to find that special soulmate. Morrison suggests that parents be prepared to help if they are needed: "Shy children, for example, can find it very hard to make overtures to a potential new friend. So you can ask if there's someone in the class they like, and make the first call for them, talking to the other child's parent to introduce yourself and make a play date. And it helps to plan something concrete and fun to do—maybe some kind of outing, for example—so the kids have an easy way to get to know each other." Teachers, too, can often help by suggesting a classmate likely to be a "good fit" for your child and maybe pairing them up on a school project or field trip.

The quality of play is changing at this age, too. "School-aged children are very rule-oriented," notes Morrison. "They spend huge amounts of time developing and negotiating 'the rules' with each other—sometimes so much that they never get around to actually playing! And there is less fantasy in their play. They still enjoy pretending, but it's less freewheeling. You have to develop the fantasy with the approval of your playmates. You can't just take your story anywhere you want, it has to fit into the shared structure of the game."

Morrison points out that while the bickering children engage in over games can be tiresome, the skills being learned are extremely valuable. Mary Marlowe, the mother of three boys, sees this growth in her oldest, eight-year-old Joshua. "My kids are very competitive with their friends; they always want to be the best. But Joshua is learning to share the limelight. I've seen real growth in his ability to work through conflict."

"This is where children learn how to co-operate, accommodate, and negotiate," says Morrison. "This is what they'll need to get along with others throughout their lives."

"HECK, NO, I WON'T GO!" NON-JOINERS

ichelle's older brothers were in hockey and other sports by the time they were four," says Mary Beasley, "and they've always been involved in activities. But when I try to enroll Michelle in things, she tells me very clearly, 'Don't sign me up because I won't go.'"

When Mary has insisted that eight-year-old Michelle take a course or join in some activity, the result, she says, "is a fight to the finish." It isn't that Michelle doesn't have any interests. In fact, when Mary noticed how much Michelle enjoyed their family swimming outings ("She was always the last one out of the water"), she was convinced that swimming lessons would be a sure-fire hit. But Michelle hated them.

There are all kinds of activities available for children aged six to eight: Cubs, Brownies, sports, gymnastics, dance, music, camps...the list seems endless. Kids who are not involved in these formal activities often create their own clubs or pick-up teams to play sports. For many kids, this is an age where "being part of a group" becomes a priority. But not every child is eager to join in.

Joanne Tee, a social worker and family counsellor in private practice in Hamilton, Ontario, explains, "In any group of kids, there are always some who are the first to jump in and be gung-ho about whatever is going on. There are some who are easygoing, and who will go along with the group. There are some who are slow to warm up—they'll take a while to feel like joining in. And finally there will be some who are just not interested in these kinds of group activities."

While all these personality types are quite normal, our society tends to place a higher value on the qualities of the extroverted and enthusiastic child.

"Teachers and leaders of children's programs are often extroverted people," says Tee. "So when they see a child not joining in, they assume there is something wrong with him, or they think he's unhappy about not being part of the group because they themselves would hate being left out."

Mary worries that Michelle will one day resent the fact that she didn't develop the skills and abilities that lessons or sports might have taught her. "Will she one day be mad at me for not forcing her to join in?"

It's possible. Tee explains that some non-joiners are really only hesitant. With a little nudge from parents, they'll end up really enjoying the activity. "It may help if you offer to go along, too, and watch from the sidelines. Or perhaps, if you have the time, you could become a Brownie leader, or an assistant coach. The reassurance of your presence may be enough to make your child feel comfortable about joining in." Signing up with a friend, or going to observe a couple of sessions before deciding, can also give kids like this the comfort zone they need.

Other children, though, really prefer more solitary, or less structured, activities. If it takes more than a nudge, and if your child is quite happy not being part of organized group activities, it may be better to let it go.

Mary finds that Michelle enjoys going along on family outings and playing with her friends in informal games. "When she doesn't sign up for any summer activities, I warn her that it will be a long summer and it could get pretty boring," says Mary, "but she doesn't worry about it at all. In fact, I think she looks forward to all those weeks of nothing to do. She's happy to play with her friends and do things with us and that's it."

Tee notes that many group activities are organized around adult expectations, with routines, rules, and objectives that suit adult needs. "Children like Michelle, on the other hand, need lots of unstructured and creative play. The non-joiner often turns out to be a very creative person."

Other non-joiners, she finds, are children with a serious and independent nature. They may find the activities planned for their age group uninteresting—they don't want to do crafts or sing action songs. Tee

ONE EXTREME TO THE OTHER: ACTIVITY OVERLOAD

In the winter season, Josh (age eight) has two hockey games a week (one in the regular league, one for the "rep" team) and at least one practice. He also has a swimming lesson every Sunday afternoon, and Cubs on Tuesday nights. His younger sister also takes swimming, as well as piano lessons and gymnastics. That's seven scheduled activities a week the family has to organize!

For every child who resists joining anything, there's another who seems to want to do *everything*. And parents often encourage this, because participating in lots of activities seems like a good thing to do. But it's easy for children—and their parents—to become overloaded with too many commitments. Throw in some unexpected homework, a birthday party, or a late meeting at work, and what started out as a pleasure can quickly become very stressful.

How much is too much? It depends partly on your child, of course. Some children can juggle more than others without showing signs of stress. But it also depends on what else is going on in the family. How many other children are also participating in after-school activities? How flexible is the parents' schedule, and how easily can they transport the kids? What will the family budget withstand? How much "free time" are you managing to spend together? Some parents find that a maximum of two organized activities per child is a workable rule of thumb, but even that may be too much in some busy families.

And if you have guilty twinges for depriving your child of a new activity, look at it this way: Self-direction and learning to structure their own time are extremely useful skills for kids to acquire. So by insisting on some down time, you're really giving her an important learning opportunity!

gives the example of an eight-year-old boy whose teacher organized regular parades for the class through the school halls and down the street. While many of the children looked forward to these parades and skipped down the halls with great enthusiasm, this particular little boy felt uncomfortable when he had to take part.

These children often flourish as they get older, when the activities become more suited to their personalities. Michelle, in fact, has recently taken up horseback riding and (much to her mother's surprise) is thoroughly enjoying it. While horseback riding is in some ways an individual sport, the lessons are given in groups and the class works together. For Michelle, it seems to be a perfect compromise between individual and group activities. Now she rides with a group of other kids every week, and, says her mother, "She likes horses so much that she's eager to go."

Tee also advises parents to be careful about signing their non-joiners up for something and then insisting they stick it out to the end of the course or year. If your child hates the program, don't force him to keep going. It won't teach him the value of finishing what he starts—it's more likely to discourage him from ever signing up for anything again, in case he gets stuck doing something he really doesn't enjoy for months.

Instead, Tee encourages parents to respect their children's personalities, and take their cues from the kids. Sometimes, they may know what they need better than we do.

THE "SLEEP" OVER: KIDS IN THE TWILIGHT ZONE

an I sleep over at Ben's house?" "Can Heather come over for a sleepover?" Parents are almost sure to hear these questions at some time during the early school years. Sleeping over with a friend is an early step toward independence, a chance to strengthen friendships and discover how things are done in other families. It can be a lot of fun for both children (and even you!), but like any new experience, it can be a little stressful as well.

Some kids head off boldly for their first sleepover without a backward glance. Others have mixed feelings. If Jordan is nervous about sleeping away from home, consider inviting an adventurous friend to stay over with you first. The opportunity to be the host helps a child prepare to be a guest.

Don't structure the time too much. It's okay to rent a movie (not scary) or plan a short outing, but the real fun of sleepovers is all that relaxed time to talk and play together.

What about bedtime? Be advised that the "sleep" in sleepover is more figurative than literal. Especially if the kids have older siblings, they may even expect to be up all night. At this age, though, most children will benefit from a friendly limit on how late they stay up. "It's a balancing act," observes Valerie Banks, a mother of two. "It's fun for them to stay up late, and useless to try to get them to sleep before they're good and tired, anyway. But if you wait too long and they get *over*tired, some kid is going to end up too wired to fall asleep and get all lonely and upset."

While Valerie leaves her older son (age 11) and his friends to fall asleep on their own ("It's a matter of going into the family room and saying, 'Okay, guys, lights out!' and then going back a half-hour later to ask them to keep the noise down," she quips), she finds that kids in this

SLEEPOVER DO'S AND DON'TS

Do:

- **Stock up on snacks (including a reasonably nutritious bedtime snack).**
- **Have some "back-up" activities (videos, board games, crafts) available.**
- **Help the kids wind down with a quiet activity at bedtime.**
- **Leave lights on for the kids to find their way to the washroom, etc.**
- **Tell visiting children it's okay to wake you if they need to.**
- **Limit the number of kids, especially for beginners (it's harder to fall asleep in a crowd).**
- **Confirm with other parents ahead of time that it's okay for their child to "bail out."**

Don't:

- **Have scary movies or games.**
- **Leave bedtime up to the kids (unless it's an unusually sensible group!).**
- **Expect kids to settle down right after a rowdy play session.**
- **Plan on an early start the next morning!**

younger age group can often use some help relaxing. "It's hard for them to wind down in a new place," she says. "I'll read them a story, or my husband will sit in the darkened room and play guitar for awhile."

If you can't count on getting a lot of sleep, you can certainly count on going through a lot of food. A quick call to your guests' parents, to check on any allergies or food restrictions, is a good idea. While you're at it, ask about any bedtime routines or fears. Some children really can't settle down without their glass of warm milk or a book to read. And be sure that any essential blankets, teddy bears, or other bedtime friends are brought along.

At bedtime, if your young visitor seems unhappy, you might suggest a "goodnight" phone call to Mom and Dad. Just hearing their voices can be very reassuring.

When it's your child's turn to be the sleepover guest, remember that she may be worried as well as excited. Will they make fun of her bedtime bear? Will they leave a nightlight on for her? What do they serve for breakfast? Good choices for a first sleepover are special "family friends"—families where your child knows and feels comfortable with the parents as well as the children. They can make the experience easier.

Discuss with her what she wants to take. If she has a blanket or teddy bear she always sleeps with, be sure it's there—and advise her hosts about any special routines or bedtime needs.

If bedwetting is a possibility, discuss the situation with your child and his host. They can protect the mattress (a clean garbage bag with a towel over it, under the bottom sheet, will work as a temporary measure) or get him up in the night if that helps. Don't forget an extra set of pyjamas.

After all this preparation, packing, and giddy enthusiasm, don't be too surprised if the phone rings at 11 p.m. and a sad little voice says, "Can you come and get me?" It often happens on the first couple of tries at "sleeping over." Let the first sleepover be somewhere nearby, for your own sake, and don't get into your PJs too early! When Marie Ouellette brought six-year-old Amy home from her first planned sleepover, she simply said, "I guess you weren't ready to sleep over yet. Maybe when you get a little older."

If you will not be willing—because of distance or other considerations—to pick up a child who has changed his mind in the middle of the night, it's only fair to make that clear from the beginning. That's what happened with Amy's second sleepover. Marie explained that she was quite willing to let her stay at her friend's, who lived on the far side of town, but she was not prepared to pick her up in the middle of the night. Did Amy still want to go under those conditions? Amy did.

When Amy called home late in the evening to say goodnight, Marie thought her voice sounded a little shaky. But Amy said everything was fine, and when Marie picked her up the next day she announced: "I had a great time!"

A final suggestion: Don't plan anything too strenuous the next day. Unless she succumbs to a nap, your young socialite may seem a wee bit testy. (You know, the way you feel after four and a half hours of sleep!) But as eight-year-old Jenny put it, "I am tired. But so what? It was worth it!"

"BUT THEIR FAMILY DOES IT":
DIFFERENT TRADITIONS, DIFFERENT RULES

ila's mom made chicken with gravy for dinner and it was so good. Can we have gravy sometimes?" "There's a baby who lives at Alicia's house but it's her sister's, not her mother's. How can that be?" "It was awesome at David's house. We were jumping off the shed roof!"

By school age, if not before, your child will be making and visiting his own friends. It's a whole new world—one that you're not a part of. And if your child's preschool social visits were pretty much limited to the children of your friends and neighbours, his new play dates with families you've never met can sometimes cause a little parental anxiety.

"It's something I've had to work hard on as the kids have grown—from having it so home-based, where you can really know everything they're doing and who they're doing it with, to letting them head off on their own," reflects Judi Hendry, mother of eight-year-old Beth and six-year-old Ben. "As they start to push out, I find it kind of scary, although it's getting easier."

Nevertheless, Judi, like most parents, feels that exposure to different families is very valuable for kids: "I think a lot of it is really exciting stuff. They learn that families do things differently, that there's no one right way. They learn tolerance, to get along with others—in fact, I wish my kids had more opportunity to be friends with people whose traditions are really different from our own."

Kate Haines, mother of four children from 5 to 15, agrees. "It broadens their horizons," she says. "Sometimes other parents will do neat things with the kids that we don't do. One family my son visits is into nature hikes and birdwatching, and has really encouraged his interest in birds. And they get exposed to other ethnic backgrounds—my daughter

VISITING MANNERS
A handful of simple courtesies will ensure your children are welcome in any family. Teach your kids to:
- **Say hello to their friends' parents.**
- **Respect the "house rules" where they are visiting.**
- **Say "No, thank you" to food they dislike, without making critical comments.**
- **Clean up toys, etc., before going home.**
- **Thank their hosts before leaving.**

Bridget has a Jewish friend whose family has involved her in their holiday celebrations."

The picture is not always perfectly rosy, though. Some family differences are great enough to cause real concern.

"Movies crop up a lot," says Judi. "We keep a pretty tight rein at home on what the kids can and can't see, and sometimes we'll be talking at bedtime and hear what they saw at someone's house and I'll think, 'Oh, my God, you watched *Terminator II*?' But I let it go—these things are part of the adventure, and not that serious.

"But then there is bottom-line safety stuff—like once I discovered that there was no adult supervision where Ben was visiting. I went right over and took him home and explained that that was not acceptable, that he simply can't go when there's no adult at home."

Kate, too, has had cause to worry about the safety of her kids. "We know of one family in particular, where there's a water danger and often inadequate supervision," she says. How does she handle it? "I talk obliquely to one of the parents—'What are you going to be doing this afternoon?'—to try to make sure there will be a parent home and on hand to keep an eye on things. Sometimes I say Solomon can go for just a little while. Sometimes I invite the kids to come to our house instead.

STAYING SAFE
As you have less direct control over the environment your child is in, it's important to start teaching some new basic safety rules. You might start with:

- Always let me know where you are.
- If you go to a friend's and no adult is there, call home.
- If the adults are drinking a lot, or acting weird, or you feel uncomfortable or unsafe in any way, call home.
- Say, "My parents asked me to check in" if you need an excuse to phone.

"And I talk to Solomon about what he's heading into—that he has to be careful, think for himself, and not just follow his friend's lead."

That's a good skill to foster early, because it becomes more and more critical as kids head into the teen years. "I tell my kids that if they ever feel uncomfortable in a situation, they should call home or come home," says Judi. "They have to know they can bail out if they need to."

Exposure to other families inevitably leads kids to campaign for "advantages" their friends enjoy—whether it's bigger allowances, more TV time, or "better" school lunches. (Funny how they don't also beg to adopt stricter table manners, earlier bedtimes, or more chores!) Judi and Kate handle most of these arguments with the time-honoured rebuttal: "People do things differently. But this is our family, and we decide how we're going to live and what works for us."

Both hasten to add that they try to be flexible about reasonable ideas and suggestions the children bring home. In fact, Kate and her husband, Andrew, have had to give some "flexibility lessons" to their kids, as well: "When Bridget (now 15) was starting school, we were vegetarians—and she found it difficult to eat at her friends' houses. We tried to assure her that it was OK to eat whatever they were having, but she was automatically critical of them—feeling that they shouldn't eat meat, and that she should tell them so. We finally went back to eating meat now and then, just so the kids would be more comfortable in other people's homes."

Whether it's adapting to a new city, a new job, or a new culture, "fitting in" is a skill that stands any adult in good stead. Kids who can visit comfortably with all kinds of families are on their way toward a lifetime of enjoying people—in all their splendid variety.

GROWING PAINS
Challenges, Theirs and Yours

EVERY AGE HAS ITS OWN SET OF CHALLENGES, and these early school years are no exception. For some, this is a relatively peaceful age, when kids enjoy family and school routines and seek approval from parents, teachers, and friends. Other children are beginning to assert their separateness in a new way. They sometimes come across as mouthy or overly aggressive, and parents struggle to deal with the problem without squelching the child's progress towards independence.

Sometimes it's the child who is struggling—and nothing is harder than watching your child have a difficult time. School, for example, can be a tough experience for some young children, and solutions aren't always easy to find. With these problems, parents have to decide when it's appropriate to step in and intervene, and when the wisest course is just to let time resolve the situation.

Sometimes simply knowing that other parents and other children have faced these same challenges—and survived!—helps more than anything else.

"I DON'T LIKE SCHOOL": COPING
WITH SCHOOL TROUBLES

I t was the strangest thing. Seven-year-old Drew seemed happy enough to go to school most of the time, but every now and then it would be a real struggle to get him out the door. It took a while for his parents to see the pattern: it was every Tuesday.

Dave Khatib, a guidance counsellor and teacher in Drew's school (St. Patrick's Community School in Red Deer, Alberta), tells this story to illustrate the wide range of factors that can lead to kids feeling anxious about school. "Only on Tuesday, he didn't want to come to school. And we're trying to find out, what's different about Tuesdays? And we eventually found out that hot lunch was not served on Tuesdays, and this child did not like eating cold sandwiches. We put a microwave in his classroom, so the child could heat up some soup and away he went, happy as a clam."

Many children resist going to school on occasion. They may have a rough few weeks at the beginning of the year, when they're getting used to new routines and new children; or they may just crave a day off now and then. But when unhappiness at school persists, day after day and week after week, that's a problem that needs solving. The first challenge is to identify what's wrong; young children, like Drew in the example above, are not always able to identify exactly what's bothering them.

"The first thing parents should always, always do, is talk to the teacher," advises Khatib. The teacher, after all, has a vital piece of the puzzle: the child's actual behaviour at school. How is she adjusting to the rules and routines? How is he getting along with other children? Does she have a special friend? Is he having difficulty academically? Has anything happened recently—a toileting accident, a stern reprimand from the yard-duty teacher, a twisted ankle in gym class—that she might be worrying about?

IS HOMESCHOOLING AN OPTION?

Lorraine Black's son Matthew, now seven, had enjoyed nursery school, so Lorraine enrolled him in kindergarten without any concerns. It wasn't until the first parent-teacher meeting in November that she realized there was a problem.

"The teacher said Matthew wasn't getting his work done, was distracted all the time, was refusing to co-operate," says Lorraine. She discovered that Matthew, a very active and energetic little boy, was being kept in most days at recess to get his work finished. As a result, she comments, "he was even more restless because he wasn't getting any exercise or play time." Frequently he was kept in at lunchtime, too.

During the summer vacation, Matthew's parents had him assessed to see if he had attention deficit hyperactivity disorder. The paediatrician who tested him assured them he did not. The following year, the situation went rapidly downhill. "My son was crying about school almost every night," says Lorraine. He continued to be kept in at recess and lunch to do his work. Matthew told his parents, "I'm stupid, I can't do anything. The other kids get prizes and stickers and I never get any."

Finally, Lorraine says, "I realized the situation was ridiculous. He was miserable, and we weren't getting anywhere. We'd tried hard to work with the school, and spent a lot of time and energy trying to make Matthew fit in, but finally we had to recognize that school is not right for him just now. We decided to try homeschooling." The improvement, she says, was remarkable. "He's much, much happier. His self-confidence is slowly coming back."

The next challenge is to find the solution, and unfortunately school anxiety can't always be relieved with something as simple as a microwave.

"One of the big reasons kids don't want to attend school has to do with peer pressure," notes Khatib. "Maybe they've been picked on, or they've been the target of some sort of ridicule."

In this situation, says Khatib, it's important for parents to work with

Like many parents beginning homeschooling, Lorraine wonders how she'll make sure Matthew learns what he needs. "But already I've been struck by how much he accomplishes now. The other day he made up his own 'math basketball' game, where he did a math problem, then shot the ball through the basket, then did another math problem, and then put the ball through the hoop again. He did that for an hour, then did another full hour of math problems on the computer. When he got stuck on a hard problem, he'd get out his Lego blocks, figure out the answer, then go back to the computer. I can see that he's really learning."

Homeschooling is legal in Canada. Some parents use one of the many correspondence courses available, some link up with other parents in a shared homeschooling arrangement, and some just go it alone. For information, contact: The Canadian Alliance of Homeschoolers, 272 Hwy. 5, R R 1, St. George, ON N0E 1N0. There are also homeschooling associations in each province that will put you in touch with local families schooling children at home, and recommend books and newsletters.

the school to "find out what happened, and what you can do to make the situation better." Khatib notes that schools are taking these concerns more seriously than in the past. "There have been so many initiatives lately, in schools, to create safe environments. We want to ensure that children are coming to a safe and caring place. Seventy percent of school-age children have been intimidated at one time or another in the schoolyard. And that's something we want to change."

At Khatib's school there is a conflict-resolution program in place to resolve difficulties students may be having with each other. Sometimes, too, Khatib will work one-to-one with children, to improve their self-esteem and peer relationships.

Most parents are not surprised when their children experience separation anxiety at the start of daycare or nursery school, but school-age children can also have real difficulty leaving their parents for the day.

Katelyn Portelli had such severe separation anxiety when she started school that it coloured her whole life. "Grade one was an awful year," recalls her mother, Lisa. "I would drag her to the bus crying and holding on to me, and begging me not to make her go. At school she wouldn't involve herself in any play or talk with the other children at recess—she would just stand against the wall. She cried frequently. And it was really affecting her physically: She wasn't eating very well, her stomach was upset, and she would have frequent bowel movements in the morning."

Even after school, there wasn't much relief: "She would come home, and she'd be fine for about an hour, but then by dinner time she'd start to worry about the next day again. She couldn't get to sleep at night thinking about it," says Lisa.

The Portellis eventually asked for Katelyn to see the school psychologist, worrying that perhaps something had happened to trigger Katelyn's anxiety. But the conclusion was that no, Katelyn was simply (or not so simply) missing her mom. "His advice was to be supportive and empathetic, and be there for her, but to keep taking her to school, and she would grow out of it."

Katelyn did grow out of it, but it was a long, difficult process that took several years and intensive support from her parents. In grade two, Lisa cut back her work hours so that she could spend time volunteering at Katelyn's school, which seemed to help. "She loved having me there and we had a deal that if I came, she would work hard and not cling to me. And she did," says Lisa. By then, Katelyn was beginning to make some friends and relax in the classroom, although the transition from home to school was still difficult.

By now, though, another problem had developed: Katelyn had fallen far behind academically. "When they're like that at school, they're not learning anything," explains Lisa. "Because all they can think about is, 'I want to go home.'" In grade three, Katelyn worked with a tutor/counsellor who not only helped her regain confidence in her school abilities, but also coached her on strategies to relieve her worry and anxious feel-

SCHOOL TROUBLES: WHO CAN HELP?
Depending on what the trouble is, you may have to draw on a number of people to support your child in school:
- the teacher—always the starting place
- the principal or vice-principal, especially for outside-the-classroom problems like bullying or if you need to request significant changes in your child's management
- school counsellor or board psychologist, to support a child with high anxiety or stress, and to consult or test for learning difficulties
- family doctor/paediatrician, especially if the child is experiencing headaches, stomach pain, or other symptoms. Troubles traced back to vision problems, allergies, or bus-induced migraines are not unknown
- outside psychologist or counsellor for individual and/or family support
- tutor or resource room teacher for one-to-one help with schoolwork

ings. Khatib feels that when children experience this kind of intense, long-term anxiety, parents are wise to seek outside counselling. "This is really more than a school counsellor can get into," he observes.

"There doesn't seem to be anything concrete you can do, though," regrets Lisa. "We were told, there are different degrees of separation anxiety, and hers is severe. You're just going to have to wait it out. Apparently it often does seem to be around grade four that it gets better."

In the face of such limited options, some parents have opted to home-school their kids for a couple of years, or even indefinitely (see "Is Homeschooling an Option?" pp. 68–69). While education professionals tend to assume that children can only resolve separation anxiety by continuing to go to school, that doesn't jibe with the experience of some homeschooling parents. Teresa's daughter Lisa, for example, adamantly refused to attend grade one. But after a couple of years of homeschooling, she announced at age eight that she was ready to go—and she was.

Katelyn's story does have a happy ending. Now in grade four, she is finally free of her separation anxiety and is for the most part enjoying school, although she does still have a tendency to worry about her schoolwork. Interestingly enough, one thing that helped was having her younger sister start school. "Christina was brimming over with confidence. Sailed right through. Loved school. And we raised them the same way," muses Lisa.

Every child is different, and we can't always predict who will have difficulty feeling comfortable at school and who will "sail through." But when school trouble does arise, careful listening to your child, teamwork with the school, and your willingness to advocate on your child's behalf are the keys to solving most problems.

BEDWETTING: DREAMING OF A DRY NIGHT

ben was a little later than average in toilet training, but was out of diapers during the day by the time he was three and a half. At bedtime, though, he still asked to have a diaper put on. A year later, he was still wet every night.

"I thought I'd try getting him to wear underpants at night," his mother, Elizabeth, said. "But he just wet the bed every single time."

By the time he was six, Elizabeth was getting concerned. Even when she restricted his drinking (no liquids after suppertime) and reminded him to go to the bathroom right before bedtime, Ben was still wet most mornings. She tried getting him up at midnight to go to the bathroom, but sometimes she couldn't wake him up enough to use the toilet, and on other nights the bed was already wet when she went in.

Shouldn't kids be dry at night by the time they're six?

Bedwetting is a common problem—more common than many of us suspect. At the age of six, about 8 percent of girls and 15 percent of boys wet the bed. Just as boys develop more slowly in other areas (they tend to be toilet-trained later, for example), they often take longer than girls to become dry at night. Without any treatment, bedwetting decreases to about 1 percent at age 15. It also seems to be hereditary— if both parents were bedwetters, the child has a 70 percent chance of having the same problem; if one parent was a bedwetter, the child's chances are 40 percent. (Ben's dad, Elizabeth discovered, wet his bed until he was about eight.)

While bedwetting may be a nuisance, it is no longer considered a symptom of some serious underlying physical or emotional problem, as it might have been a generation ago.

"In the past, we gave any child who was referred for bedwetting a pretty extensive investigation," says urologist John Hambley. "Now

COULD IT BE A MEDICAL PROBLEM?
About 3 percent of bedwetting children have a medical condition or anatomical abnormality that is causing the problem. In most of those cases, though, other signs are apparent as well, such as daytime wetting, repeated urinary tract infections, or other symptoms. A urinalysis can rule out kidney problems or infections and is certainly in order if your child has been dry at night for several months, and then mysteriously resumes frequent bedwetting.

most of these cases are not even sent to a urologist, and the doctor will simply do a physical exam and urinalysis to rule out physical problems. In most cases, it's simply a matter of slower-than-average development."

Dr. Norman Wolfish, of the University of Ottawa, describes three factors that he believes are important in bedwetting.

One is a bladder with an "infantile pattern of contractility." A baby's bladder contracts frequently on its own, and when the bladder becomes full, the contractions become stronger and the urine is released. As children mature, this changes and they develop the ability to control the release of urine. For some children, this pattern of involuntary contractions persists much longer—especially at night.

The second factor is an anti-diuretic hormone produced by the body, which seems to be at low levels in bedwetting children. Babies produce urine at about the same rate 24 hours a day, but adults have higher levels of this hormone in their systems at night and that reduces their nighttime urine. Some children take longer to develop higher levels of this hormone and so continue producing large amounts of urine during the night. As Dr. Hambley comments: "When these kids wet the bed, it's not just a little trickle, they really flood things."

A new medication, taken as a nasal spray, is a synthetic form of this hormone and can reduce nighttime urine production to help the child stay dry. Many physicians have found this drug quite successful. It does

WHEN TO "DO SOMETHING" ABOUT BEDWETTING
The Canadian Paediatric Society suggests that bedwetting shouldn't even be diagnosed—that is, identified as anything unusual—until after age five for girls and age six for boys. After that age, they suggest, the best rule of thumb about treatment is the *child's* feelings, since training treatments work best when the child is strongly motivated to try them. (And, on the other hand, the great majority of children will gradually grow out of bedwetting even if you do nothing.) So if your school-age child is upset by his bedwetting, and wants help to stop, it might be time to talk with your family doctor or paediatrician.

not work on all children, however, and the bedwetting tends to return once the medication is discontinued. Dr. Hambley finds it is often most useful for sleepovers and camping trips—those times when a wet bed can be most embarrassing.

The third factor noted by Dr. Wolfish is an area he has been researching. "We studied boys aged eight to twelve who were bedwetters and tried to find out how difficult it was to wake them when they were asleep." The researchers discovered what the parents of bedwetting kids have been saying for years: "These kids are extraordinarily difficult, if not impossible, to wake up."

Dr. Wolfish explains that all of us have an "arousal threshold" for being wakened from sleep. In babies and very young children, this is normally quite high, but as children mature the level gets lower and it takes less to wake them up. The bedwetters, however, continued to sleep very deeply and were hard to wake up—even when the researchers activated buzzers at 110 to 120 decibels (that's as loud as a household smoke alarm), only 14 percent of the bedwetting children woke up.

This research, Dr. Wolfish feels, is important because it makes it clear that bedwetters "are not being lazy, are not doing it on purpose to upset their parents. They simply have no control over this—they can't wake up!"

So what does the parent of a bedwetter do? Dr. Hambley points out that "This is a laundry problem, not a health problem. Most children will outgrow it even if you do nothing at all." At least at the earlier end of this age group, wearing the underwear-styled overnight "diapers" designed for older kids is a convenient, if pricey, solution.

There are also a number of treatment regimens that can be discussed with your physician. These include alarm systems that wake the child as soon as he begins to urinate, medications to reduce urine output, and exercises to strengthen the bladder-control muscles and increase the bladder volume.

Perhaps the most important part of treatment is maintaining a positive attitude. Yes, wet beds can be annoying, but it's important not to blame the child or embarrass him over something he simply can't control. Use a plastic cover to protect the mattress, and keep a clean towel and pyjamas beside the bed so he can easily change if he gets wet during the night.

It's also important to pass on that positive attitude to your child. Reassure her that bedwetting will be outgrown, and that "it's no big deal." If she's invited to a sleepover or slumber party, talk it over with her. Perhaps this is a good time to use some medication, if your child's doctor recommends it. Or perhaps you simply need to have a private talk with the parents involved, to make them aware of the problem and what precautions they might take (because bedwetting is so common, you might discover that they already have experience with this).

And what happened to Ben? After the doctor examined him and found everything to be normal, Elizabeth decided just to wait. As he got older, the percentage of wet nights gradually decreased, and by the time he was nine, they had become quite infrequent. Shortly after Ben's tenth birthday, Elizabeth realized she hadn't changed a wet bed in months. As most children will, Ben had grown out of bedwetting.

PEOPLE ARE NOT FOR HURTING:
TAMING AGGRESSIVE BEHAVIOUR

ben and his brother Sam are chasing each other around the front yard, waving wooden swords in the air. When Ben catches Sam, he ties him to a tree with his sister's skipping rope and threatens to cut off his head. Two minutes later, Sam is untied and telling Ben he's going to capture him with his magic fire-thrower (a foam cup he has coloured orange).

Jacob and his sister Dawn like to wrestle and "play-fight." When Dad comes in to see what the screaming is all about, they tell him not to worry, it's just playing.

Alex often provokes fights with the other kids at school. When Randy refused to share one of his toys, Alex grabbed it away and broke it, then laughed when Randy cried. Alex has also been cruel to the family cat, stepping on her tail deliberately and throwing her in the air "to see if she'll land on her feet."

Ben, Sam, Jacob, and Dawn are probably within the normal range of behaviours (although Ben and Sam seem to have been watching a lot of TV!).

But Alex may be having problems with aggression, according to guidelines from child psychologist Sarah Landy, who runs a program for parents of children showing aggressive behaviour at the Hincks Centre for Children's Mental Health in Toronto.

What are some of the aggressive behaviours that might lead parents to seek help for their families? Landy suggests that parents consult with a professional about a school-aged child who regularly:

Hits, bites, scratches, and throws things when he becomes frustrated.

Is cruel to others and lacks empathy for the needs and concerns of others.

Deliberately hurts animals for no particular reason.
Destroys toys and other property.

Early intervention for the child displaying overly aggressive behaviour is very important, Landy explains, because almost 50 percent of young children with this kind of behaviour will continue to have problems as they get older and may, according to research studies, eventually get into trouble with the law.

Social worker Linda Maxwell has also helped many parents whose children had these problems in a program (now discontinued) that she offered in Simcoe, Ontario. Maxwell says, "It's normal for kids to chase, wrestle, and play-fight, and it's normal for two-year-olds to hit each other over the head with toys. But when the motive of the child is not to have fun but to hurt, there is a problem, or if the child is still hitting other kids over the head at age six, parents should be concerned."

Landy emphasizes that dealing with aggression in children is not just a matter of finding ways to stop a particular behaviour. "The tendency has been just to deal with the behaviour. But this is more than star charts and time-outs—there are all sorts of underlying reasons why a child has these problems, and we need to get at these."

Her program is 20 weeks long and, as she points out, "is quite complex." Parents learn about child development and ways to teach their children the skills they need to deal with anger, solve problems, and improve their relationships. As Maxwell says: "Everybody has some degree of aggression, everyone feels angry and frustrated at times. In my practice, children learn other ways to express their feelings—through physical activity, art, writing, or making things with play dough. But just teaching anger management can be like putting a Band-Aid on a cancerous tumour—you need to also treat the underlying causes of the child's problems."

What are the underlying problems? Landy explains that there are many different possible causes, and often the parents need to look at

WHAT ABOUT TV?

Child psychologist Sarah Landy feels strongly that an overdose of violent TV shows can lead to increasingly aggressive behaviour in children. "Children learn from these shows that the way you get what you want is through violence. It becomes casual, normal, acceptable. I think our whole society has too high a tolerance for violence and aggression, and children naturally absorb this."

Research studies do suggest a link between violent TV and aggressive behaviour in children. While there are many socially well-adjusted children who do not "act out" the violence they see on television, kids who are already showing problems with anger or aggression may be especially vulnerable to violent images. Limiting the amount and monitoring the quality of TV-time, especially for these kids, not only reduces their exposure to a potentially harmful influence, but frees up their time for more creative play.

making changes in several areas. She adds: "Many parents get into a self-defeating cycle. The child acts up, the parent wants to stop the behaviour so he punishes the child, the child feels rejected and hurt so she acts even worse, the parent punishes more severely, and it goes on and on. What we try to do is break the cycle by suggesting some different approaches."

One idea: "Setting aside a short time (ten or fifteen minutes) two or three times a weeks to just play with the child. The child chooses the game or activity, the parent just follows the child's lead. This helps to create a more positive relationship and can reduce the stresses in the family." It sounds deceptively simple—most of us already spend more time than that playing with our kids. But making that focused, enjoyable, one-on-one time together a priority can really make a difference.

Maxwell suggests that parents who are concerned about aggressive behaviour should consider restricting TV-watching (see above sidebar), encouraging active play, and making sure they model positive behaviour

THE TROUBLE WITH TEASING

It can be incredibly painful for a parent to witness his or her child being teased. The wounds inflicted by teasing can't be cured with a Band-Aid or a kiss, yet we'd love to find a way to protect our children from the pain of other children's words.

That's probably impossible, says Joanne Tee, manager of Counselling Services at Family Services of Hamilton-Wentworth. Teasing is very common from around age five and continues right into the teen years. Almost all children are teased at some point, and those who are "different" in some way may endure more than most.

How can parents help a child who is being teased? "It's important first that you demonstrate that you like them for who they are. Offer comfort, not criticism. If your son is being teased about being fat, for example, this is *not* the time to discuss diets and exercise."

She suggests instead saying something like, "People have to like you for who you are, not how you look." You might also help the child think up some responses, such as "I don't like it when you call me that, and I won't play with you anymore if you say it again." Tee adds that the parent must then be prepared to play with the child or help him find other ways to fill his time, if the teasing doesn't stop.

It can be just as tough to handle the situation when your child is the one doing the teasing. Tee reminds parents that "Kids don't tease for no reason. The child who teases is feeling hurt, angry, left out, or unhappy about something, and it may have no connection with the child who is being teased. Often an older child will come home from school after a bad experience there and tease a younger brother or sister. It had nothing to do with the younger child; the older one is just putting the younger one down because he feels put down."

She suggests that parents need to respond first to the feeling of hurt or anger that underlies the teasing. "If you walk in on your child teasing another, don't start yelling and getting mad. Let him know you're supportive and care about how he's feeling. Help him identify feelings—say 'You seem really angry.'"

That doesn't mean, she adds, that you should "allow" or ignore the teasing. At a later time, when the situation is calmer, parents can bring up their concerns: "I don't like it when you tease; it hurts the other child's feelings." Remind him of a time when he was teased, and how it felt. You can also point out that teasing is likely to cost the child playmates.

If your young child teases someone about a disability or a different religious or ethnic background, some education is in order. A book or two from the library, a rented video about another religion or country, a visit to a place of worship that is not your own—all of these could help your child learn that differences should be valued, not condemned.

Joanne Tee emphasizes that while parents cannot entirely eliminate the pain of being teased from their children's lives, giving them solid support and the assurance that they are loved for who they are goes a long way to reducing the impact.

in their own relationship with the child. Giving extra physical affection when their child's behaviour seems to be deteriorating is often helpful.

Both Maxwell and Landy emphasize the need to seek help if the problem continues. "If you are worried, if you think there might be a problem, you should talk to a mental-health professional about your child," says Maxwell. "This situation will be much more serious and harder to deal with when your child is 16 and 6 feet tall."

"IN THIS CORNER…": TEACHING FAIR FIGHTING

he weather was good, the kids got to play with the new baby piglets, and all in all we'd had an enjoyable visit at my parents' farm. But now came the final hurdle: the long drive home.

We're no more than an hour away from the farm when it starts. Somebody gets poked. Danny's looking out of Jeremy's window. Jeremy's hogging all the crayons and won't let Danny use the red one. Before long, a full-fledged battle breaks out, the older two kids are taking sides as well, and I'm desperately looking for a place to pull off the highway.

But we don't have to be in the car for the kids to start fighting. They do it at home, in the playground, in shopping malls; they fight with siblings, cousins, friends, and classmates.

John Macmillan, from Family Services of Peel, says, "If you have more than one child, you are almost certain to have fighting."

But he sees a good side to the squabbles that drive parents crazy. Children fight because they are learning how to interact with others, he explains, and learning to "fight fair" will help them deal with other people. Parents can help that process and reduce the actual fighting—by teaching their children problem-solving skills.

"The kids need to know what to do when they get mad," Macmillan says. "You can ask the child who is upset, 'What do you want to happen?' If she says, 'I want him to give my toy back,' ask her what she thinks will work. Calling names? Threatening? Give her a sense of what it's like to be in the other child's shoes."

This approach teaches kids to negotiate rather than hit. Macmillan recommends arming children with a whole list of things they can do besides hitting.

"Help them to express their feelings by really listening to them and

FIVE TECHNIQUES FOR DEALING WITH CHILDREN'S FIGHTS
In Nancy Samalin's book, *Loving Each One Best*, she summarizes the approaches parents most often find effective when it's time to intervene in children's fights (most commonly, siblings, but friends, classmates, and cousins, too):

- **CONSEQUENCES:** Usually for everyone involved, not just the most obvious aggressor—as in, "Whoa! No hitting! Everyone take a cool-off time in their rooms."
- **CLARIFICATION:** Rather than over-generalized commands like "settle down" or "be nice," try being more specific: "I need you both sitting quietly in different chairs before the TV goes on." Samalin suggests "impersonal, concrete statements about what you want."
- **NEGOTIATION:** This won't work when kids are furious at each other. But if they're relatively calm, try "You guys work this out—with words." You can add, "Let me know what you agree on, and if you need help, I'm here."
- **DISTRACTION:** Do they really have to work through a fight about who ate the most peanuts? No! They need to drop it, and get on with life. Intervene with a snack, an activity, or a joke—or simply separate them.
- **EMPOWERMENT:** When a sobbing child comes to you for comfort after teasing or insults, it's tempting to jump in and condemn the insulter. But you might do better to bolster her own self-confidence: "Are you stupid? I don't think so either. Look how well you read, and how quickly you figured out that puzzle. Aaron shouldn't call you names, but if he does, you don't have to believe him."

checking back that you understand what they're saying. You can say 'It sounds like you're really mad about this.' That does two things—it lets the child know he's been heard, and it gives him the vocabulary to describe his feelings."

Of course, before the child can speak coherently about the problem, he or she has to calm down. It's easier to calm the child, Macmillan says,

"I'M TELLING!"

While "tattling" is extremely common in this age group, in the long term it's not a habit most parents want to encourage. It drives you crazy to have every minor transgression reported to you (and instantly denied by the accused), and not only that—you also want your child to learn the skills she needs to deal with problems on her own.

On the other hand, you *do* want your child to report to you when the situation is dangerous or too much for her to handle. Too often, for example, we hear of children who endured years of bullying because they didn't want to "tattle." Those kids really needed adult protection. How can we help kids sort out the difference between "tattling" and "telling?"

Debby Wright, who became the stepmother of four children five years ago, says because kids this age are so big on rules, she finds the best way to deal with tattling is to make a rule about it. "Ours is that we don't tell on others unless they're hurting themselves or someone else, or the situation is dangerous."

Grade two teacher Susan Clarke discusses with her students the difference between tattling and what she calls "reporting." Tattling, she points out to the students, is generally done to get someone else into trouble. But reporting an important situation might prevent or limit trouble—"if a child is in danger, for example."

Most commonly, though, a child will complain that another child hurt him or took one of his belongings. "This can sound like tattling, but really it's a request for help in dealing with a situation," says Clarke. "I see it as a valuable opportunity to teach children the skills they need in dealing with other kids." Her first response in that situation would be to ask the child what steps he had already taken to solve the problem. If he hadn't even talked to the others involved, Clarke would send him back to discuss the situation. Only if the children couldn't resolve the situation on their own would Clarke step in to help.

if you are calm yourself. Put you hand on the child's shoulder, or give him a little hug, and suggest: "Take a deep breath." Once he's back in control, you're ready to discuss the problem.

On the other hand, parents should not intervene in every fight. In fact, paying too much attention to fighting can, in Macmillan's opinion, actually encourage it. He recommends commenting frequently on the times when they play well together and work out their differences.

So when should parents intervene?

"First of all, there is such a thing as a play fight. If they're both wrestling around and nobody seems upset, it's probably just play and you can ignore it," says Macmillan. "And if they're working things out themselves—even if it's getting fairly heated—they're learning important social skills, so stay out of it. The time to intervene is when one child is in danger of being hurt, either physically or emotionally."

That can be a fine line, and Macmillan points out that you have to know your child—an insult that bounces off one child can be devastating to another.

When one child does insult another, and you need to intervene, Macmillan suggests saying: "I'd never want anyone to call you that name, so I don't want you to call your sister that." Responding that way reminds the "insulter" that you care about him, even though he's done something you aren't happy about.

Parents also need to give clear messages about fighting. It's valuable to state clearly that "people are not for hitting," to remind your children to "use words, say what you feel," and to teach them to negotiate—but children are also carefully watching how parents handle disagreements. You may want to monitor your own "fair fighting" skills.

What about the backseat battles that went on between my kids dur-

RECOMMENDED READING

Some parent helpers in the "This squabbling is driving me crazy!" department:

Siblings without Rivalry: How to Help Your Children Live Together so You Can Live, Too, by Adele Faber and Elaine Mazlish, Avon Books, 1987.

"Stop It, You Two!" 90-minute audio book by Kathy Lynn, Parenting Today, 2762 Wall Street, Vancouver, BC V5K 1A9.

ing the long drive home from my parents' farm? Macmillan remembers a car trip when his three youngsters started fighting. He suppressed the urge to take a swipe at one of them and pulled off the highway onto a little-travelled concession road. The kids all sat there silently, wondering what was going to happen.

"I guess you've been cooped up in the car too long," Macmillan told them. "And you need some exercise. So start running, and I'll follow along behind you."

While the children ran along the grass shoulder, he drove slowly, keeping his car between them and the traffic. (Don't try this on a major highway!)

"It wasn't a punishment," Macmillan stresses. "They really did need to get rid of some excess energy. And by the time they got tired and climbed back in the car, they were laughing and relaxed, and we drove a long way without any more problems."

As Macmillan demonstrated, applying a little creativity to the situation can reduce fighting. But we shouldn't expect to eliminate it. "Fighting is part of learning life skills," Macmillan points out. "There are some things you can only learn by doing."

THE TRUTH ABOUT FIBBING: WHY KIDS LIE

Six-year-old Michael comes home from school and announces that he is the best reader in the class. You know he hasn't really mastered reading yet and you can't imagine that this announcement is the truth.

Seven-year-old Hannah comes out of the kitchen with a guilty look on her face. When you go in to check, one of the cookies you had cooling on the counter is gone. "Did you take a cookie, Hannah?" you ask. She denies it, but you know she's lying.

Why do children tell lies? In his book *Why Kids Lie*, author Paul Ekman gives four main reasons: to avoid punishment or getting into trouble; to get something they want; to avoid hurting others; or because they've seen others lying (most especially their parents).

But Joanne Gusella, a clinical psychologist at the Izaak Walton Killam Children's Hospital in Halifax, says it isn't quite so simple with children between the ages of six and eight, because they still often find it difficult to tell the difference between fact and fantasy. She quotes one study that found only 18 percent of six-year-olds reliably knew the difference; it wasn't until children were nine that the majority understood that Cinderella and giants were not real, for example.

Gusella also cites research on the stages of moral development: "Children in this age group are in the pre-conventional stage. That means that what's right or wrong is determined by the consequences. If the consequence of telling a lie seems better than the consequence of telling the truth, the child will be strongly motivated to lie."

Because she takes this developmental perspective, Gusella thinks parents often become unnecessarily alarmed when they catch their child in a lie.

Gusella offers some suggestions for encouraging honesty. "First,

TELLING TALL TALES

One little boy is the source of much amusement in our family for his imaginative narratives. They aren't so much lies as embellishments: "Oh, yeah, Ryan went to a wrestling match one time, and one of the wrestlers walked right by him, and Ryan's dad put out his hand to touch him, and the wrestler flipped him right into the aisle ..." Where does truth end and fantasy begin? We're never quite sure.

Are we worried about this child's moral development? Not at all. He doesn't lie to get other children in trouble. Nor does he boast and exaggerate his own prowess, or demand to be the centre of attention. He's a nice, well-behaved, well-liked kid with, I believe, an honest love for a good story. He just enjoys going where his imagination leads him.

Some kids tell a lot of "tall tales" because they have a need to escape their reality, or because they are desperately hungry for attention. These kids need help. But if your child is happy and functioning well, there's no need to be alarmed if she enjoys dramatizing real life. After all, that's what the great novelists do. Maybe you just have a budding Margaret Atwood (or Steven Spielberg) on your hands!

remember that kids are like tape recorders—everything they see and hear is taken in and eventually played back. If you have been telling little white lies—pretending your six-year-old is only five so you don't have to pay full fare on the bus, for example—your child will get the impression that lying is OK."

Putting a lot of pressure on a child may also inadvertently encourage lying. When Michael tells his parents he's the best reader in the class, it may be his way of trying to live up to their expectations. He very much wants to be a good reader, so he pretends he is and hopes to please his parents by telling them about his fantasy. It's important to let your child know you love him as he is, and that you will be happier to hear the truth, even if it's less impressive.

The child who feels trapped may also lie. If you're certain that

Hannah took the cookie, don't question her. When she sees that you are upset, she'll be even more tempted to lie. It's better simply to state that you know she took the cookie, and explain the consequences (she'll get no cookie after supper, for example, when the rest of the family will be having dessert).

"If your child is lying frequently, you need to discover the reason for the lies by thinking about what happens afterwards," says Gusella. "Is your child lying to avoid punishment, or to impress others? Each of those situations would need to be dealt with differently."

Children often "stretch the truth" in order to impress their friends or family, she says. In those situations, Gusella likes to tell the child the story of *The Boy Who Cried Wolf*. "It's a great way to get across in an indirect way the point that others will stop believing you if you lie to them."

If you suspect your child lies in order to avoid punishment, you might ask yourself if your punishments have been too severe. A better approach may be to reward telling the truth. For example, if you ask your children who spilled the grape juice on the white carpet, and your eight-year-old son admits that he did it, you can say: "It must have been difficult for you to tell the truth, especially when you could see that I was mad. I'm really impressed. I'll come and help you clean it up." Your words plus your willingness to help him clean up will give him a positive reason to tell the truth next time.

It's also important for parents to provide good role models of honesty by demonstrating that quality in their own lives. In Ekman's book, he admits: "[one] week...I carefully watched my own behaviour. I caught myself telling eight lies, two of them to my children. They were the kind of lies that were not serious. For example, I told the meter maid that I had just run into the store for a minute."

But the child observing that behaviour may not find it easy to understand why your lies are OK while hers are not. If you can lie to the meter maid to avoid the punishment of getting a ticket, why, she might well

CHEATING

Cheating is a behaviour that can go hand in hand with fibbing, and early-school-age kids may be especially susceptible to the temptations of an easy out.

Parent educator Kathy Lynn comments that occasional cheating may just be an "experimental behaviour" that never resurfaces. "But if cheating seems to be an ongoing thing—something your child is relying on—you need to think about why your child is cheating." Cheating in school—copying another child's homework answers, for example—particularly warrants your attention (and a discussion with the teacher), because it may mean the child genuinely finds the work too difficult or is having trouble organizing and remembering his work.

Kids at this age are often strongly drawn to board and card games, yet many still find it very hard to handle losing. And when they get together, of course, they all want to win, so cheating can become a very heated issue. Some suggestions:

- If the players are mismatched, consider evening the odds at the beginning. An adult playing chess with a child may agree to giving up a few pieces. Teams can be evened up by pairing up older and younger kids.
- Alternatively, take the focus off winning and losing by creating a co-operative version of the game. Try for the highest "group score" in Scrabble, for example.
- When kids' games start to deteriorate into accusations of cheating and tearful denials, Lynn suggests offering a choice: "Tell them they can either work things out between them or just not play any more. Sometimes the kids will decide to change the rules to suit them both, and that's OK. But other times you just have to put the game away quietly and encourage them to find something else to do."
- As your child heads into the next age group, competitive games will be popular, while "poor sports" and "cheats" will not. If your eight-year-old cheats so frequently that it causes social problems with her peers, you might want to get some advice from a school counsellor or other professional.

wonder, is it wrong for her to lie about taking the cookie to avoid being punished?

"Children are not just small adults," Gusella reminds parents. "It takes time for them to understand the concept of honesty and to learn to be truthful. They need our help in developing those qualities, and we may need to change our own actions in order to be good role models."

TANTRUMS REVISITED: THE
MELTDOWN, SCHOOL-AGED STYLE

You've probably heard about the Terrible Twos and the years of teenage rebellion. But there's another age when parenting can be a little more stressful than usual. As international speaker and author Barbara Coloroso explains: "At two, children rebel against their mothers. At five or six, they rebel against their parents. At puberty, they rebel against the entire adult population."

Hearing that was a great relief to Rita Braeden, who had wondered if her daughter Liza was the only almost-six-year-old who seemed to have undergone a dramatic personality change. "We had certain routines and expectations in our family, and Liza had been co-operating with them since she was three or four," says Rita. "But all of a sudden, at age five and three-quarters, she'd refuse to make her bed or even hang up her jacket."

These things, Rita says, hadn't been a problem for several years, and it surprised her when formerly routine tasks became battlegrounds. "Liza would be snappy about the least little thing, and if I asked her to do something simple—like hang up her coat—she said I was picking on her, that I didn't love her, and there'd be tears and tears and tears," Rita remembers.

Sometimes it seemed to her that Liza was breaking every rule she could think of. She didn't want to brush her teeth, she didn't want to go to bed at her accustomed bedtime, she argued over every small request. Getting ready for school in the morning was also a source of constant stress, as Liza seemed to move "slower than molasses on a cold day."

"She also would ask for something over and over, sometimes 50 times in a row, even though I kept telling her she couldn't have it, or that she had to do something else before she could have it, and that just drove me crazy," says Rita.

CAUTION: TANTRUM IN PROGRESS

It's hard enough to deal with a two-year-old kicking and screaming on the floor. But at least a toddler doesn't take up the whole hallway! School-age tantrums are definitely trying, but a combination of sympathy (for the feelings) and firmness (about rules and limits) will get you through.

Some strategies other parents have used:

- Ignore it. With some children, simply ignoring the tantrum works best, even if you have to go into another room to do it. Having an audience just seems to egg them on. Once the fury has blown over, you can see whether your child needs comforting or to just get on with life.

- Physical contact. Some children can use some adult help in getting control of themselves. A hug or your hand rubbing their back or arm—maybe just your calm presence—seems to stabilize them.

- Nip it in the bud. A tantrum-in-the-making can sometimes be deflected with gentle humour (not mean-spirited teasing or imitating!) or by being offered an alternative: "Whoa, boy! Don't freak out on me! Would you rather have a shower in the morning instead of tonight?" Once the tantrum's in full swing, though, this approach is probably counterproductive (read on).

- Don't reward the tantrum. Even at this age, tantrums are usually genuine expressions of frustration and anger rather than deliberate attempts to manipulate a parent. But if the parents *are* swayed by the sound and fury—"Oh, just stop that hollering, will you? If it means that much to you, I guess you can stay up a while later"—well, the temptation is obvious. Instead, ride it out, dry his tears, and give him a hug goodnight.

- Get help if the tantrums are scary. Yelling, crying, flinging herself onto the couch, stomping up the stairs—it's not pretty, but it's normal. But if your child is breaking things, hurting herself, or trying to hurt you, consider asking a professional for help in dealing with these angry outbursts.

Rita realized that she was becoming overwhelmed by these struggles with her daughter and her reactions had simply become automatic. When she stepped back a bit and looked at the situation, she was able to unravel some of the causes. One was the demanding adjustment to grade one.

"Liza's teacher told me she was well-behaved in school, was a good listener, and followed the rules well. This was the complete opposite of the way she was behaving at home. I decided that maybe she was feeling tired—and tired of being good—when she got home from school, because that was one of our worst times."

Rita began preparing a nutritious snack for Liza to eat as soon as she came home, and then giving her a little time to relax on her own. She also tried to make mornings easier by allowing Liza some options. For example, she'll make Liza's bed for her if she doesn't have time, but it costs Liza 25 cents from her allowance.

"I try not to let these minor issues escalate into huge battles," Rita says. "And while we still have some tantrums, it's not with the same intensity."

Not all children Liza's age will assert their independence so vigorously. Research by Dr. Stella Chess of the New York University School of Medicine suggests that some children are simply born with tantrum tendencies. The high-intensity child, she explains, responds to everything with greater energy and is more prone to tantrums. These children even have different physical responses to stress, which suggests to Chess that the personality difference has a biological basis. Her advice: Try to be aware of the situations and circumstances that are likely to trigger an outburst, and either avoid them or prepare to ease the child through them.

Barbara Coloroso adds that with a child like Liza, who is not compliant at age six, parents will often find that independent nature a positive trait when their daughter becomes a teenager. She's not easily led by her parents now, and she will probably not be easily led by her peers when she becomes a teenager.

While Rita found it helpful to know that temper tantrums are common at Liza's age and in children with her personality, those blow-ups can still be difficult to deal with. "Mothers get tired at the end of the day, too," she points out. Rita tries to remember that this stage—like others—will pass. She remarks, with philosophical humour, "Like a lot of stages, just when you think you can't stand it any more, just when you're ready to give them away to the first family that's willing to take them, it comes to an end."

The important thing, she adds, is "getting through it without wrecking your child's drive for independence or knocking down their self-esteem—or your own."

THE DEATH OF A LOVED ONE:
SAYING GOODBYE

eath has different meanings for children of different ages. The preschooler lives in the "now" and can't really understand that the person who has died is not coming back; weeks later the three-year-old might ask, "When's Grandma coming over?" But after about age five or six, children are able to understand the permanence of death, and they will mourn the loss of a friend or relative much as adults do.

"Death is a natural part of life," says Rudy Kopriva of the Kopriva-Taylor Funeral Home in Oakville, Ontario. "When someone who has been close to a child dies, the child will grieve. That's natural, too, and we encourage parents to give the child a chance to say goodbye."

Should parents bring children to funeral? Yes, in most cases, says Kopriva. The funeral is a special opportunity for saying farewell to the person who has died, and children can really benefit from being included with the rest of the family in that farewell. "We even have a playroom in our funeral home with videos and games for children, so that they can take a break if the situation is becoming too difficult for them. That's how strongly we feel about including children," he says.

Myrna Renshaw, executive director of Bereaved Families of Ontario, Halton/Peel Branch, maintains that "children should be included as much as they want to be. They should be told about what will happen at the funeral, and given the opportunity to attend if they want, but they should never be dragged there if they don't want to go."

How close the child was to the person who died will be a significant factor in making these decisions. If the deceased is a parent, sibling, or other very close relative, the child should be given the opportunity to be involved as much as possible. Otherwise there may be feelings of resentment and regret that can last for years. If the child

WHEN A PET DIES

It may seem trivial compared to the death of a person, but the loss of a pet is often felt deeply by children. Moreover, it is likely to be their first close brush with death. And in a way that's not a bad thing. A child who sees the still, limp body of his gerbil or guinea pig and helps bury it in the back garden learns first-hand about the finality of death without the trauma of losing a close relative. But it still hurts. How can parents help?

- **Allow your child to grieve in his own way.** To you, it may have been a stupid goldfish that she never paid any attention to anyway. That doesn't mean she won't be upset by the sight of it upside down in the bowl. If she's sad, she needs to be sad.

When our old dog had to be put down, each child responded differently. My oldest son (and I) cried—a lot. My middle son, age seven, got very busy with his baseball cards and hardly seemed to react. He did his crying weeks later, and experienced several weepy bedtimes. My youngest wanted to talk a lot about Jay—he seemed to be trying to fix his memories of her—but didn't seem to be as saddened as the other two.

- **Allow him *not* to grieve, too.** He may *not* be deeply affected, or not right away. That's also okay. Some kids identify closely with animals, some don't.
- **Answer her questions as honestly but gently as you can.**
- **Help him find a way to say goodbye.** When "Mr. Newt" died, my eight-year-old son held a little funeral in the back garden, with the girls next door in attendance. It was a brief but dignified ceremony, with a few tears shed, followed by a bracing snack.

was not as close to the person who has died, she may not want to be as actively involved.

Of course, when a close relative dies, the parents may be so upset and busy coping with their own grief that dealing with a child becomes very difficult. As Renshaw observes, "It's not unusual to see a parent so overwhelmed with grief that he or she either feels unable to meet the children's needs or hopes to somehow shield the children from the sadness. Well, it's impossible to shield them. And I think parents should resist the temptation to send them away to be cared for by someone else. They need to be part of the grieving, even if you have to enlist an aunt or uncle or other person to help care for the children and answer questions."

No matter what his relationship was to the deceased, your child will probably have dozens of questions about death.

"Children need to have their questions answered simply and honestly and probably need to hear the answers more than once," says Renshaw. "When you explain something, they will go away and process the information, and then come back with more questions."

Most funeral homes offer brochures, booklets, and videos to help parents respond to the concerns of children. Kopriva, for example, provides a brochure called *Helping Children Understand Death* (with an introduction by Mr. Dressup), a colouring workbook entitled *Saying Goodbye* that describes funerals and provides spaces for the child to draw memories of happy times with the person who has died, and a 15-minute video called *Children and Death*, among other guides.

Renshaw suggests a few other tips to help children cope with funerals. "If the casket can be open, that is often helpful to children. When the casket is closed, the child's imagination takes over. With an open casket, a parent can show the child that the person looks almost like he did before, but not quite, and that he is really dead, not breathing, not moving." Jill Krementz, author of *How It Feels When a Parent Dies*, has also noticed, based on her interviews with many children, that having an open casket seems to help the child deal with the reality of death. Of course, children should never be forced to view an open casket if they'd prefer not to.

When Penny Riker's daughter died after a brief illness, the hospital staff urged her to bring her younger children in to see the body. She resisted. "I knew my kids, and I knew it would upset them." Eventually, the staff persuaded Penny to bring them in. As she recalls, "They wouldn't go near her, and they were both just sobbing and crying, but when I look back now I think it was the right thing to do. It did help them to understand her death." She decided to have a closed casket at the funeral because she felt many people would be upset at seeing a child in an open casket, and she found that decision easier knowing the family had said their good-byes at the hospital.

Parents who are worried that the emotional intensity of a visitation or funeral may be too difficult for their children can ask for a private visit before others arrive. That gives the children a chance to say goodbye without coping with a crowd of grieving adults.

However, Renshaw points out that attending the visitation—even if it is only for a short time—can sometimes be very helpful for kids. "They see that other people are sad, too, and that it's OK to cry. And they often feel supported by the presence of others who also cared about the person they have just lost."

Children can also be helped to say goodbye in a way that is meaningful to them. One child may want to write a letter and put it in the casket; another might draw a picture of himself and the person who died. Parents could help put together a scrapbook or folder of photos and other mementos of the deceased. Some families have planted trees or flowers in memory of a deceased relative, and this can be an excellent way to involve children in commemorating their loved one's life. Some kids

BOOKS TO HELP CHILDREN COPE WITH DEATH

FOR ADULTS:
How It Feels When a Parent Dies, by Jill Krementz, Alfred A. Knopf, 1988.
Lifetimes: The Beautiful Way to Explain Death to Children, by Bryan Mellonie and Robert Ingpen, Bantam Books, 1983.

TO READ WITH CHILDREN:
The Fall of Freddie the Leaf, by Leo Buscaglia, Holt, Rinehart and Winston, 1982.
The Three Birds: A Story for Children about the Loss of a Loved One, by Marinus van den Berg, Magination Press, 1994.
Why Did Grandma Die? By Trudi Madler, Raintree Steck-Vaughn, 1992.

might prefer these activities to attending the funeral, but many will want to be part of the ceremony as well.

Renshaw points out that in her experience, people are beginning to recognize that children do have a place at funerals. "If parents take the time to prepare them and help them through the process, a funeral can be a very valuable way of helping a child say goodbye to someone they love who has died."

PLAY ON!
The Value of Play in Middle Childhood

SOMETIMES PARENTS THINK THAT ONCE children start school, they've outgrown play. Building with blocks or playing with dolls is fine for preschoolers: they are learning skills they'll need for school. After grade one, though, children may be urged to focus on learning, not play.

But play is important throughout childhood. Even adults need to play, and for six- to eight-year-olds, it's vital. Play helps a child relax after a stressful day at school (and trying to behave and pay attention all day can be very stressful!). Children continue to learn through play, to work out their concerns and emotions, and to practise adult roles.

The typical child's day of school, chores, sports, and other commitments needs to be balanced with plenty of unstructured play time. Yes, computer games and hockey practice are "play"—but they won't meet your child's need for play that *he* chooses and directs himself. Helping your child maintain that healthy balance will make these years better for both of you.

"I'M BORED": WHAT TO DO WHEN THERE'S NOTHING TO DO

"'m bored." Those words again. You know they'll be followed by "and there's nothing to do," and already you're dreaming up a list of possible solutions. But before you rush to find some entertaining activity for your youngster, consider that a little boredom might actually be a good thing.

Kathryn Brink, mother of six, grade one teacher, and author of the *Hamilton Spectator's* popular "Parenting" column, emphasizes the need for children to take responsibility for filling their own time. "Parents can end up standing on their heads to entertain a child. Instead, you need to show him how to take control of his time and find interesting things to do."

How do you teach that lesson? Kathryn suggests that during your less busy times, you sit down with your child and make a list of "great, fun, exciting ideas." (Chores don't count.) This can be pulled out when the doldrums hit. You might also encourage your child to poll his friends on what *they* do when they get bored. (Of course, calling friends may lead quickly to some joint activities, which solve the boredom problem.)

Kathryn also encourages parents to model good problem-solving skills in their own lives. "Say in front of the children, 'I'm feeling bored today, so I think I'll try this or that.' Let them see how you deal with it."

If a child complains of boredom frequently, it might be a good idea to look at his environment. Is there too much emphasis on keeping the house tidy—no potentially messy activities allowed? Are there friends or siblings around? Are there enough creative toys to play with, or supplies for crafts and games?

Having the right supplies on hand makes it easier for your child to cook up some play activities on her own. A dress-up box of old clothes can spark many games, and an art box of paper, crayons, markers, and

YOUR CHILD'S INSPIRATION SHELF

If you keep some or all of these items on a shelf or in a big cardboard box, your child might find some of them inspirational when he or she has "nothing to do."

- A deck of cards (or two)
- Jigsaw puzzles
- Games (especially those that can be played by one, like dominoes)
- A set of magnets
- A magnifying glass and a jar to catch bugs in
- A flashlight
- Stamps and an ink pad
- Puppets
- Interlocking blocks (Lego) or other construction materials
- Paper and crafts materials (toilet paper rolls, glue, glitter, etc.)
- Sidewalk chalk
- Word search, dot-to-dot, and other easy puzzle books
- An assortment of balls, from tiny super-bouncy balls to beach balls
- Old catalogues
- Maps you don't mind kids writing on
- Activity or crafts books: Klutz Press makes spectacular activity books on everything from friendship bracelets to shadow animals, but there are many others in bookstores and libraries.

Add other items to reflect your child's special interests, and be sure to change the items from time to time.

any crafts materials you can come up with (old toilet paper rolls, scraps of fabric, foam containers, etc., plus purchased items such as glue, Scotch tape, glitter, and coloured tissue) will inspire the child who likes to "make things."

Many children of this age are beginning to join groups such as Beavers and Brownies, and to sign up for lessons and sports. Kathryn finds it works best to limit her children to two activities each (for example, Brownies and baseball, or swimming and music), to avoid overscheduling. However, she says, "We try to introduce them to as many different things as possible over the years. That way they have more options to choose from when they're looking for something to do, and I think having choices is important in reducing boredom."

Boredom can sometimes be a step on the way to a new creative activity, to inventing an absorbing game, or to discovering a new interest. Parents who can avoid jumping in too fast to alleviate boredom, instead encouraging children to seek their own solutions, are often delighted with the results.

Leslie Perkins has noticed that although her six-year-old doesn't always say "I'm bored" out loud, he often has times when he seems restless. "Jonathan will finish some activity, and then I notice him pacing around and looking tense. That's the boredom stage. It isn't long, though, before he's off building something in the basement or quietly playing with his toys. It's like the boredom is a transition time before he thinks up something new to do."

Kathryn agrees. "Feeling bored is a signal to get yourself in gear, to get involved in something," she says. She believes parents can help their children learn appropriate responses to that signal, so that boredom is replaced by activity.

EVERYBODY WINS: CO-OPERATIVE AND NON-COMPETITIVE GAMES

n our highly competitive society, is there still room for games and activities that teach children to be co-operative? Definitely, says Nadeane McCaffrey, Director of the Free to Be Me Camp in Ottawa, Ontario.

Based on the writings and philosophy of Terry Orlick, a Carleton University professor of sports psychology and the Canadian guru of co-operative sports and games, the camp takes children between the ages of three and twelve and creates for them a non-competitive, positive environment.

In competitive games, McCaffrey points out, one child wins or achieves the goal at the expense of the other children. So while that child may feel pleased about succeeding, all the others feel discouraged about failing. Non-competitive activities allow everyone to succeed (or fail—because sometimes the group's goals are not achieved), and encourage the concepts of working together, sharing, and helping others.

Jamie Davidson, the father of Jared, Kieran, and Noah, tries to integrate the ideas of co-operation in all the things he does with his sons. "I think my whole way of being with them is co-operative, rather than competitive or challenging. Many of the things we do together aren't real games but we're still working together. They like to help me fix things, for example, or we'll cut wood together."

The four of them often go for nature hikes with the common goal of finding something new each time that they haven't seen before. "Last week we found a salamander with eggs for the first time—*I* hadn't even seen salamander eggs before!" Jamie remembers. "We have a joint collection of plants and rocks that we all add to when we find new things on these walks."

Another favourite co-operative activity is building marble runs. "We have built millions of marble tracks together," says Jamie. "Part of the fun is trying to find things that marbles will roll on—pieces of wood, some toy wooden railway tracks, plastic, whatever we can find—and then putting the track together. Then we roll the marbles. The kids just go crazy over this, they really love it."

Jamie has also adapted traditional sports to reduce the competitive aspects. He plays co-operative baseball—without keeping score—with his sons and their friends, where each player simply rotates to a new position after hitting the ball. Everyone gets a chance to play in each position, including being the pitcher and being up at bat.

They also play what Jamie calls group tag, where instead of one person trying to catch all the others, the person who is "it" runs and is chased by the entire group. (Kids love to be chased!) When "it" is caught, another person gets a turn to be chased.

A favourite indoor game is balloon tennis. "We try to see how long we can keep the balloon up in the air, so the goal is to hit it so the other person can return it to you, not so they can't. Sometimes we play this lying on the floor on our backs and using our feet as well as our hands to keep the balloon from touching the ground."

Many other games can easily be adapted to co-operative play. At birthday parties, co-operative musical chairs is often a favourite. The adult in charge sets up the chairs and stops and starts the music as in regular play, but when a child can't find a chair to sit on, she isn't out—she just sits on someone's lap. By the last round, a dozen or so children are trying to sit on just one chair. It leads to lots of laughter—and keeps everyone involved.

Anne Perkins, the mother of five children, plays only co-operative games at her children's birthday parties. "We have no winners, no losers, no prizes—unless everyone gets a prize. None of the kids has ever complained. In fact, I think it's made birthday parties more fun."

Some traditional board games are equally adaptable. In co-operative Scrabble, players work together to get the highest group score on each

CO-OPERATIVE RESOURCES

The Second Cooperative Sports and Games Book, by Terry Orlick, Pantheon Books, 1982. A collection of great co-operative ideas.

Feeling Great: Teaching Children to Excel at Living, 3rd edition, by Terry Orlick, Creative Bound (1-800-287-4414), 1993. More co-operative and esteem-building activities.

Both titles, and information about the Free to Be Me Camp, are available from: Feeling Great, PO Box 20395, Ottawa, ON K1N 1A3.

Everybody Wins! Non-Competitive Party Games and Activities for Children, by Jody L. Blosser, Sterling Publishing, 1996.

Family Pastimes makes co-operative board games. Available in specialty toy stores, or for a free catalogue, write to: Family Pastimes, RR 4, Perth, ON K7H 3C6; 1-888-267-4414.

round. Instead of trying to bury helpful letters to beat your opponent, the strategy focuses on creating opportunities for the other players to add high-scoring words. You can create a co-operative Trivial Pursuit by not using the board and just taking turns asking questions.

Jamie believes that fostering co-operation is a very important part of parenting. "You have to recognize that if you include children in your activities, if you get them to help you make or fix things, there is going to be some mess and the quality of their work may not be up to your standards. But it's worth it to have them involved."

As another example, he describes how his sons love to run races. "They plan out a route, and then run one at a time while I time them. I encourage them to try to beat their own best time, not to be trying to beat each other. If Jared says he's faster than Kieran, I'll say, 'Yes, you're very fast for a seven-year-old and Kieran is very fast for a four-year-old.'"

When her children do want to try more competitive activities, such as races, Anne creates handicaps for the older ones. For example, in a race her oldest son might have to hop on one foot while the younger ones can run. This takes away some of the competitive aspects and adds to the fun.

COMPETITION WITHOUT TEARS?

Leanne Clark's son, seven-year-old James, loved gymnastics—until his coach suggested he enter his first competition. While Leanne expected he'd enjoy the excitement, James couldn't think about anything but winning, and when he placed fourth he dissolved into tears. On the way home, he told his mother he didn't want to do gymnastics any more.

Many of the sports and other activities children want to participate in have a competitive aspect. How can you make the experience as positive as possible?

- Encourage your child to think about improving himself, rather than comparing to other kids—achieving a higher score than last time, swimming faster than before, or stopping more shots than in the previous game.
- Talk about the fun you expect to have at the game or competition. On your way to the baseball game, you can speculate about which of her friends might be playing on the other team.
- After the event, talk about your child's accomplishments, good teamwork, and other highlights. Let him see that winning isn't important to you.
- In organized team sports, look for a league or organization that has each child play for the same amount of time. That shows a focus on participation, rather than giving the best players most of the action so that the team can win.
- If competition is clearly taking the fun out of the activity for your child, look for alternatives.

That's what Leanne did. She made an agreement with James that he would go back to gymnastics, but it would be up to James when (or if) he entered another competition, and she let the coach know their plan. Although the coach disagreed with her approach, he went along with it—and James is once again enjoying his time in the gym.

McCaffrey, through her work at the Free to Be Me Camp, has seen how learning co-operative play can benefit children from a wide variety of backgrounds. "I started out working with children who were very gifted athletically, and we've also worked with children who had cancer and who had problems such as ADD (Attention Deficit Disorder) at our camp. They all benefit from the same principles of learning to work together with others, learning to relax, learning to co-operate, and being positive. These concepts increase self-esteem and teach social skills."

GO FOR THE GUSTO: THE JOY OF ROWDY PLAY

Teresa had arrived for a visit. Her seven-year-old, Jeremy, came along to play with my seven-year-old son, Riley. And did they play! For the better part of three hours, they roared in and out of the house.

They never walked when they could run, talked when they could shout, or sat when they could hurl themselves in a heap of struggling arms and legs. Several times we had to intervene—"No water squirters in the house!" "Out of the living room—we're trying to talk!" "Watch out for the younger kids." But the play never turned nasty, and nobody (miraculously) got hurt.

The grownups were a little frayed around the edges by the end of the visit. But the kids glowed with exertion and satisfaction. On the ride home, Jeremy asked his mom if she had been mad at him.

"Not mad, exactly. But you guys were pretty rowdy at Holly's house," she replied.

"But Mom," explained Jeremy patiently. "That's just the way boys have fun!"

"Rough play has probably been a part of childhood since the beginning of time," reflects Diane Prato, a parent educator and counsellor specializing in family issues. And while it does seem to appeal more often to boys, Prato believes "it's a very positive experience for kids of both sexes."

Positive? When the noise and energy levels rise, it can be hard for a parent to feel very positive about it. But Prato points to several benefits of roughhousing.

"In our society, we're used to verbal communication. Roughhousing is another kind of interaction—'body contact' interaction. It allows a child to develop his body awareness, to learn about his physical strength and limitations. He's able to enjoy his body in contact with another in a non-sexual way. It's a healthy way to reduce stress and let out pent-up feelings. Plus, it's fun!"

"Play-fighting" is probably the form of rough play that parents have the most trouble with. "It will end in tears!" we pronounce (like generations of parents before us), and all too often, it does. But pretend fighting among "consenting children" is not a hostile activity.

"I think it's partly an expression of affection," muses Angela Summer, a single mother whose three children (two boys and a girl, ages nine, eight, and six) enjoy "all kinds of rowdy play, but especially wrestling." She observes that older kids who may not feel comfortable hugging each other, for example, get a chance to get physically close rolling around on the floor together. Trust is an issue, too: Would you play-fight with a kid who might really clobber you?

It takes self-control and skill to engage in wild, abandoned play while still being aware of looming dangers, and most children can't manage it for long. That's why Prato suggests that parents need to set and enforce ground rules about rough play. Some issue to consider:

Where is roughhousing allowed? You'll want to set limits for safety (not on the top bunk!), to protect your things (not near the china cabinet), and possibly to protect your nerves (not underfoot). "When possible," Prato suggests, "outdoors is safest."

How can a child stop the play? Anyone who has raced outside to rescue a shrieking child, only to find her laughing with her friends, realizes how hard it can be to distinguish real panic from exuberance. Teach your children to use some kind of code—'Time-out' or 'Uncle' or 'Stop!'—that must be instantly honoured.

Does everyone get to "win" sometimes? Younger siblings may be bossed into games that condemn them to be forever squashed on the

TIMID KIDS

Anne's older son, Glenn, loved active and boisterous games. He'd sometimes leap on his dad's back as soon as he came in the door, and in minutes the two of them would be wrestling on the floor.

But while those wrestling games were under way, their younger son, Adam, would stand on the sidelines and watch. "Adam never liked rowdy games," Anne says. "His dad would grab for him, and he'd just back away."

While many kids enjoy rowdy play, some don't. Anne comments that we rarely worry about little girls who don't want to wrestle and roughhouse, but boys who are equally unwilling to "mix it up" may meet with disapproval and pressure to join in. Adam also didn't share Glenn's love of sports, but preferred quieter, less active games.

In Adam's case, his dislike of roughhousing was simply a difference in personality. Some children, however, become overly fearful of physical injury, avoiding both "body contact" play and other physical challenges like climbing and balancing. Sometimes this stems from having been warned repeatedly, "You'll get hurt!" whenever they get too exuberant or lively. If that's the case, you might need to make a point of encouraging your child to take small risks, and censor the urge to add safety cautions. If you get right in there and wrestle, swing, or chase, too, that's a great way to send the message that this kind of play can be both safe and fun.

bottom. Prato suggests we teach the "underdog" ways of being more assertive—perhaps putting his hands out for protection and yelling, "No! I don't like that!" Give the older one the responsibility to negotiate rules the smaller child is happy with: "It has to be fun for both of you or you can't play." My middle son has come up with his own solution—he'll play superheroes with his older brother, "but only if we're both on the same team."

No "weapons." Sticks, toy swords, and anything else that can be thrown or poked make the risk of serious injuries much higher.

Finally, Prato suggests, parents should be aware of how the play is progressing. "You don't want to hover over them constantly, but do check in periodically to make sure the ground rules are being respected. And consider setting a time limit. This kind of play often deteriorates. Call a halt and change the pace—perhaps offering an alternative like a snack—before it ends in total chaos or someone getting hurt."

When Angela's kids do "lose it" ("Pretty much every time," she admits wryly), she separates them. "I put them in different rooms, to let everyone cool off. They have to find something quiet to do, like reading."

Prato encourages parents who feel comfortable doing so to join in with their kids. "As a child, I didn't experience much rowdy play. But my husband did, and he roughhouses with our two girls,"

Angela says, "My kids love it when I wrestle with them. We often do it after supper, when we're all together. And when I'm involved, I can show them how to keep it safe."

"It's amazing how they've changed and grown stronger," says Angela. "But," she grins, "I still always win."

CALLING CLOUD NINE: IN DEFENCE OF DAYDREAMING

hildren's author Sylvia McNicoll of Burlington, Ontario, is a staunch defender of daydreaming. "As a fiction writer, I often daydream about the stories I'm working on or ideas I'm developing," she says. "People talk to me and it takes a while before I can pull myself back to reality and answer their questions. But daydreaming is an essential part of the creative process."

McNicoll is a frequent speaker in schools and often watches for the "daydreamy" children, encouraging them to express their creativity during her workshops. "Sometimes the teacher hasn't seen these children's strengths and thinks they are just withdrawn or not paying attention."

When McNicoll invites a dreamy child to plot a story or create a character, "the child may suddenly perk up and amaze the rest of the class with her talents." She remembers inviting one little girl to create a storyboard for a picture book and was very impressed by the detailed and elaborate tale she came up with. The girl's classmates were clearly surprised—and impressed—as well.

The daydreamer's talents may not be in story writing, though. McNicoll remembers a friend's son who loved to build with blocks and Lego and take his bike apart and put it back together. When he seemed to be in another world he was often imagining the next structure he would build or figuring out how to repair a minor glitch in his bike.

Sharon Degraw recalls that her daughter Jennifer would "talk to herself, sing to herself, walk down the street in her own little world. I'd look out the window and see her walking along, making gestures, and nobody else was there."

Jennifer daydreamed at home, in the car, while watching TV—even at school. Fortunately, her teacher was understanding. "She encouraged Jennifer to sing the songs she made up to the whole class, and Jennifer

IS IT ATTENTION DEFICIT DISORDER?

By now most people have heard of "attention deficit hyperactivity disorder"—ADHD. This is a condition characterized by difficulties in focusing attention, distractability, impulsivity, disorganization, and sometimes physical restlessness. Unfortunately, the "hyperactive" face of ADHD is the most noticeable and widely known, so that many people assume the child with attention deficit disorder is always fidgety and loud.

Not so. As Barbara Ingersoll notes in her book, *Daredevils and Daydreamers: New Perspectives on Attention-Deficit/Hyperactivity Disorder* (Doubleday, 1998), some children with ADHD are actually "somewhat sluggish and underactive in general tempo, and parents and teachers describe them as absentminded daydreamers and space cadets." What distinguishes these children from the child who just has a "dreamy personality" is that they really *can't* pay attention and organize themselves in structured settings like school, even when they try.

The difficulty, from a parent's and a teacher's point of view, is that it's not easy to distinguish the child who is simply not interested in schoolwork from the child who tunes out because she doesn't know how to tune in. To make matters more complicated, many children with ADHD can focus very well on activities they find stimulating, whether that is a Lego set, a video game, or an art project—which adults, naturally enough, tend to take as evidence that "you *can* concentrate if you try."

If your child is struggling and discouraged in school, and you suspect that an attention problem may lie at the heart of his difficulties, first do some reading (Ingersoll's book is a good, up-to-date introduction, but there are many other titles available). Then, if your concern is still there, ask to have your child assessed. There are both medical and behavioural ways to support a child with ADHD, but often the most positive change of all is the change in attitude teachers and parents experience as their understanding of the child grows.

actually liked performing. After that, when I noticed her lost in her own world, she'd tell me 'I'm rehearsing my songs.'"

Some teachers, however, can find daydreamers a challenge. Marilyn

Vance has been teaching in Peel Region (Ontario) for over a decade. "I get frustrated when children are dreaming in class because they're missing out," she says.

She sees several causes for what she describes as "excessive daydreaming" in children. One occurs when kids are overloaded with too many structured activities. "Some kids are just involved in too much. They need some down time and they end up taking it in school." These children, Vance feels, need to have their schedules pared down to a manageable size so they have time to relax and just sit and think. Very persistent dreaminess in school, Vance feels, can be a sign of other troubles, from boredom or lack of understanding to problems at home. In cases like these, she may try to meet with the child—and sometimes his parents—privately to see what can be done.

Most daydreaming, however, is not problematic. "It's usually just the right half of the brain trying to solve a problem," McNicoll says. "It may be creating a story, reviewing an experience the child has actually had and is trying to make sense of, or planning a future activity. But it is often very important and valuable to the child."

Irene Pallar's daughter Sarai (now 12) was a confirmed daydreamer by five. After having watched Sarai all these years, Irene believes that "it's a private thing. I'll sometimes ask her what she's thinking about, but she usually says 'nothing' so I don't press her." When Sarai does share her daydreams, they're often "what-ifs" like, "What if we lived in a castle instead of our house and I was a princess?" or "What if I was in the Olympics and won the gold medal?"

McNicoll agrees that parents should tread lightly when asking about their children's fantasy lives. "Their daydreams are truly their own— they might share some of them with us, but most of the time we have no idea what they're really thinking. When you're a child, most of the time you have adults telling you what to do, when to do it, and how to do it. Daydreams are the place where the child is in charge."

VIDEO GAME ADDICTS: THE LURE OF THE ELECTRONIC SCREEN

arents often buy an expensive new toy wondering if their child will play with it enough to justify the price. When they buy video games, however, they may have the opposite concern: Will the child play with it too much?

The image of the junior video game addict, glued to the screen hour after hour with his little hands clamped to the controller, haunts many parents who have succumbed to pleas for a video game set. Is their concern justified?

Ann Wordsworth, a researcher for CBC's *Marketplace* program, examined the phenomenon of video games for one episode of the show. She believes there may be cause for concern. "It has been compared to a gambling addiction, because the games offer the same kind of positive reinforcement, rewards, and increasing levels of difficulty to children that gambling offers to adults," she says.

Rose Dyson, of C-Cave (Canadians Concerned about Violence in Entertainment), says, "Kids become absorbed by it. And I think we should be concerned about the content. The games tend to be based on competitiveness, blowing things up, killing the bad guys. About 75 percent have very high levels of violence."

Wordsworth agrees. "Some of these games teach terrible values. It's quite instructive to really look at them and be aware of what's going on."

Some of the popular "quest-type" games, for example, are less violent but have very sexist themes. As my daughter, Lisa, said: "I'm really tired of rescuing princesses."

Of course, not all children who play video games become addicted to them. Computer expert Sherry Turkle is quoted in *Mothering* magazine as saying: "Most people don't become addicted to video games, just as most people who diet don't become anorexic. Of course, some people come to the material more vulnerable than others." She believes that children who feel powerless in their own lives may be strongly attracted by the feeling of power video games give them.

Some children who initially spend hours zapping away become bored with the games after a few weeks. Their interest may revive temporarily if they get a new game, only to drop off again once that game is mastered. Other kids continue to play but don't overdo it; for them, video games are just one of many fun things they enjoy.

But for those children who remain absorbed by the games, Dyson is concerned. "It takes them away from the playground, physical exercise, reading, playing actively with their friends—it can eat up so much of their time."

How can parents tackle the problem?

Wordsworth feels that it's best to set rules from the beginning. "Parents often buy the game system as a reward or a present, and then if they start trying to restrict or control it, that's seen as a punishment." Better that it start off, like the TV, as a family possession controlled by the parents.

Setting rules early on was also the key to avoiding problems for the parents who tested video games for the Canadian Toy Testing Council. Their experiences are described in a generally positive report in the 1991 issue of the *Toy Report*.

Dian Nease, mother of three boys and owner of one Nintendo set, sums up the feelings of most "Nintendo parents" when she says: "I feel kind of ambivalent about it. Some days it's okay and some days I could chuck it out the window."

It's a great way to keep the boys occupied when she needs to, and Dian often hears them laughing or cheering together when they've accomplished something. That's the good side. She's less enthusiastic about the times when they ignore homework or other responsibilities to play the games, or when they get grumpy about any interruption.

Dian points out there are plenty of non-violent games. Some are

COMPUTERAMA

Six-year-old Claire loves her "Living Books" CDs and can spend hours clicking on different elements in the illustrations to see what they'll do.

Seven-year-old Jeremy plays his older brother's computer games whenever he can. He loves anything that involves shooting bad guys, aliens, or weird creatures, and really gets involved in some of the role-playing games.

Eight-year-old Luke has been struggling with math. His dad brought home a computer game that disguises math problems with lots of action and sound effects. For Luke, it's a pretty painless way to learn those number facts he's had trouble memorizing.

There's an old joke that if you can't get your computer to work, ask any seven-year-old to help you out. There's definitely some truth to it; because children don't have the fear of new technology that adults often struggle with, they're willing to dive in and experiment with a new game or program.

With a huge range of computer games available, here are some tips to help you choose good ones:

- Educational games should have a strong game element if you want your child to stay interested. A program that simply does an on-screen fireworks display every time she gets the right answer to a question will soon become boring. One that asks her to add the numbers on a present and direct Santa to deliver it to the right house makes the problem-solving part of the game.
- Just as many video games are violent, so are lots of computer games. Read the description on the package carefully!

re-creations of sports events—baseball, football, hockey, track and field, etc. Some let you be a game-show contestant—Wheel of Fortune and Jeopardy are popular. Tetris and Dr. Mario have no obstacles or villains, just a series of shapes that the player must twist, turn, and manipulate into the winning pattern. Little Nemo Dreammaster has obstacles and wild animals, but the animals aren't killed—they have to be "tamed" by feeding them candy. Once tamed, they will give Nemo rides through the

- While younger children enjoy repetition, children in this age group are beginning to prefer novelty. A game that allows for many variations and alternative scenarios will be more appealing than one that is always the same.
- Ask to try the game in the store to be sure it is easy to use. While children are often more intuitive about mastering these games than adults, they quickly become frustrated if they can't control the characters or figure out the next step.
- Encyclopedias and other information CDs can also be a great learning resource for your child. Again, it's important to check them out in advance, as some require more advanced reading ability than others.

Finally, don't forget that a computer, whether used for games, homework, or personal learning, is still an electronic screen. Children who rotate from video game to computer to TV can give the impression of doing varied activities, when what's really happening is hours sitting in front of a screen. Those are hours your child is *not* playing outside, drawing, reading, inventing and acting out detective stories, learning to knit, etc. Keep an eye on your child's total "on-screen" hours, and don't let them eat up her day.

hazards on his route. At the other extreme are games with very graphic violence, so parents do need to be aware of what they're buying.

Having a video game in your home brings up many of the same issues as having a television. Parents need to make decisions about how long children can play and what games are permitted, just as they need to supervise TV-watching.

But be warned! Parents, too (often in a doomed attempt to keep up with their seven-year-old), have been known to join the ranks of video game addicts.

BURPS, BUMS, AND BANANAS:
CHILDREN'S HUMOUR

 f laughter is the best medicine, then young children must be a healthy lot. And it's true that the ability to take pleasure in laughter and a lively sense of humour are great cushions against stress and difficulties at any age.

Young school-agers, though, are in a bit of an awkward stage as far as humour goes, and it's not always easy for adults to appreciate their high spirits. Well past the age when almost anything they said was "cute" and their laughter irresistible, but not yet able to remember and recount (or even, often, to understand) adult-style jokes, kids at this age can try our patience with what seems to be pointless silliness:

We have visitors, and the dinner table is a crowd of boy cousins, ages six, seven, eight, and ten. The mood is high hilarity, with all three younger boys erupting in helpless laughter so frequently that I'm afraid someone will inhale their food. (I needn't worry—no one is eating.) What's so funny? Anything, apparently, that my oldest son does, from breathing to scratching his head. Just as things start to die down, a timely burp sends everyone into new hysterics.

Rude noises and scatological words do, of course, figure high on the list of clever humour for primary school kids, especially (let's admit it!) the boys. (I know a seven-year-old boy who spent so much time cupping his hands behind his knees and "farting" out the trapped air that the tops of his calf muscles became sore!) Other childish amusements can appear equally lame to us adults. But if "Jingle bells, Batman smells" doesn't captivate you, the level of development that your child's glee reveals just might.

Jennifer Hardacre, an education professor at University of Toronto's Institute of Child Study who has a special interest in play, points out the many cognitive achievements that go into, for example, understanding a joke: "Jokes play on ambiguity and the unexpected. To 'get' them, we have to be able to classify objects and words, sequence actions, understand what is possible and plausible and what is not, recognize and enjoy incongruity. We have to realize that some words have two or more meanings, and be able to hold both of those meanings in our mind at the same time."

Children in the primary grades, says Hardacre, just happen to be going through "the big shift" in their cognitive development that will allow them to appreciate this more adult-style humour.

"Most children entering this period enjoy very broad humour—they laugh at things like physical pratfalls, unexpected visual elements (like putting underwear on your head), or silly sound combinations," she explains. "Six-year-olds have the notion of a joke, that's it's supposed to be funny—but they often haven't really grasped what makes a punch line 'work.'" That's why your six-year-old likes your knock-knock joke, but then counters with one that doesn't "make sense." She hasn't quite mastered the verbal play of this particular form:

"Knock, knock."

"Who's there?"

"Slug."

"Slug who?"

"You eat slug sandwiches!" (har, har, har)

By eight, though, most children understand and enjoy puns, riddles, and jokes. Unfortunately, they have probably also mastered—and/or been on the receiving end of—sarcasm, mockery, and teasing:

"I'm Laura," announces your three-year-old.

"No, *I'm* Melissa!" refutes her seven-year-old big sister.

"No, I mean *I* am Laura!"

"I know you mean I. And *I* am Melissa!" (hee, hee, hee)

So Laura's in tears, and Melissa thinks she's pretty clever. Now what? Hardacre suggests we avoid an angry "How would you feel?" lecture. Even if Melissa is experienced enough to predict the effect of her words,

FROM HUMOUR TO HORROR: THE FASCINATION WITH FRIGHT

When Ann Leon's son Gabriel turned six, he developed a fascination with the notorious Goosebumps books. Even though he couldn't read yet, he insisted on borrowing a couple of volumes from the series every time he went to the library. Then he'd take them up to his room and look at the scary pictures. "I think it was like a badge of honour," Ann says. "He was making a statement—that he was big enough and brave enough to have these scary books."

Gabriel's seven now, and loves to watch "Goosebumps" on TV as well as read the stories.

Why do many children in this age group like to be frightened? "It's the thrill," says Colleen Francisci, the mother of seven-year-old Sammy. "It's sort of a luxury for kids to enjoy being scared. These scary books and movies are something they can control—they know they're safe and secure even as they enjoy a few vicarious thrills."

Unfortunately, by around the age of eight the horror genre is so "cool" with some groups of friends that there may be pressure to watch scarier shows than a child is ready for. "Getting through frightening movies can be a way of demonstrating to themselves and to their friends that they're brave and tough. And when it's over they tell everyone, 'Oh, I wasn't scared,'" observes Colleen. Then some poor kids go home and have nightmares about dinosaurs or aliens.

What's important here is to stay aware of your child's responses, not what his group of friends enjoys. Each child is different, and those who are more imaginative and sensitive need more protection from scary material, even if they really want to see it.

odds are she will protest, "It's just a joke! That wouldn't bother me!" Instead, Hardacre suggests more emotionally neutral feedback: "That's not funny for Laura. It makes her feel frustrated and hurt. Please don't tease like that any more."

Just as important is Hardacre's suggestion that we take a good look at our own use of humour, and make sure we're modelling what we'd

You can help by not allowing him to watch things you *know* will be too much (it's easier for a kid to grumble about his mean parents than to admit to his friends that he's scared), by finding him less intensely scary stuff that he *can* handle, and by watching with him and "coaching" him through. "Sammy will sometimes want to watch something scary on TV, and he'll tell me to turn off the lights and be all excited about it," says Colleen. "Then after it starts he'll say 'Mom, don't leave.'" Knowing Mom is there to keep you safe can give a child that comfort zone that allows them to enjoy—rather than endure—the scary parts.

Kids who share the fascination with monsters, frightening rides, and spooky stories that is common at this age aren't likely to grow up with unusually morbid interests. They're just getting their feet wet in a world that can be pretty scary, especially when you're not quite eight years old.

like to see. "Many adults do tease children about their immaturity," she observes. "It's very easy to fall into—children are such easy targets. But because they are literal in their thinking they will take it seriously."

The difference between laughing *with* and laughing *at* is a good one to keep in mind. If Julie, trying out a word she's read but never heard, announces, "I'm so excited I'm on *tender hooks!*" will you laugh? Unless she's very sensitive, sure you will. It's funny. But sarcastic put-downs, gleeful repetitions of the story in her presence, or relentless harping ("So, are your hooks tough or tender today?") is humour at the child's expense. This does not teach kids to be resilient, says Hardacre; it just makes them feel vulnerable and humiliated.

On the other hand, modelling how you can gently laugh at *yourself*, or find the funny side of a bad experience, is good for everyone in the family. (But not, Hardacre hastens to add, the harsh self-putdowns that sometimes masquerade as humour.) Martin Seligman, author of *The Optimistic Child*, notes that this ability to see the humour in our everyday foibles promotes good mental health.

Sharing in our children's high spirits, enjoying their laughter, laughing easily ourselves, all encourage the development of a healthy sense of humour. But you don't have to fake it or allow burping contests at the table, if that's not your thing. The world is full of potential humour, and plenty of it can be shared by old and young alike.

NEVER TOO OLD: READING TO THE EARLY READER

t seven, Sam Gleason is just beginning to enjoy reading simple stories on his own. Does he have a favourite book? "*The Hobbit* and *The Lord of the Rings* are my very favourites. I loved *Treasure Island* and *Sword in the Stone*, too. Oh, yeah, and *Robinson Crusoe*."

Obviously, Sam didn't become so well-read all by himself. His love of books—substantial, challenging books at that—is a direct result of the hours his parents—and especially his dad—have spent reading to him. "Being read to, and reading himself, are completely different activities for him," notes his father, Jim. "Being read to is one of the highlights of his day. If I'm going to be out at bedtime, Sam and I both make sure to reschedule a reading time together."

Maitland MacIsaac is co-author of Making Connections, a program designed to teach parents strategies to assist their children with learning and reading. He refers to reading aloud and storytelling as part of an "oral tradition" that is vital to becoming an effective reader.

"The four components of language—reading, listening, speaking, and writing—are interconnected: Speaking enhances writing, listening enhances reading, etc. Reading aloud helps the speaking/reading connection," says MacIsaac, who works with a non-profit organization called Learning & Reading Partners Adult Learning System in Charlottetown, PEI. And when parents read their child well-written books, he observes, it allows the child to hear a sophisticated, masterful use of language—language, if you like, used to its full potential. "This exposure is important, because day-to-day speaking tends to be dialogue, short or incomplete sentences, one-word responses, that sort of thing," observes MacIsaac.

Reading aloud is a family tradition for mother of two Katherine Orgill. "I remember my mother talking about how her dad used to read

FIRST NOVELS TO READ ALOUD
Looking for a place to start? Here are some titles, old and new, that our children have enjoyed. Some are short and sweet, others a little more challenging:

The Adventures of Captain Underpants, by Dav Pilkey, Scholastic, 1997. Fast-paced, easy to read, and endearingly silly, with plenty of funny illustrations and even a section of "flip action" pages, this is an easy step up from longer picture books.

Bubsy, by Don Lemna, Riverwood Publishers, 1993. Another fun read, about a boy with big-brother problems.

From Anna, by Jean Little, Fitzhenry & Whiteside, 1982. A well-loved classic about a little girl who immigrates to Canada from Germany.

The Giant Baby, by Allan Ahlberg, Penguin Books, 1994. Young Alice's attempt to keep and care for the *huge* baby that's left on her family's doorstep is very funny and appealing.

The Iron Man, by Ted Hughes, Faber & Faber, 1985. A powerfully written story, simple enough for a six-year-old, but good enough for almost anybody.

to them," she says, "and I have good memories myself of being read to at age seven or eight." Even now, when their children are ten and thirteen, Katherine and her husband occasionally share a book with their kids. "One thing I like about it," says Katherine, "is that you can read stories that would be difficult for them to read themselves. I see it as a way of encouraging that level of reading."

Katherine observes, though, that children's tastes and abilities vary here, as everywhere else. "We read the Narnia series to Emily starting at about age five, but Cameron wasn't ready for it until he was eight years

Mouse Tales (The Mouse Who Wanted to Know, A Message from a Mouse, and others), **by Anne Merrick, Raincoast Books, various dates. A charming series of stories about a family of house mice with irresistible names, like Alacrity, Serenity, Curiosity, and Oddity.**

Owls in the Family, **by Farley Mowat, Bantam, 1985. Another Canadian classic the whole family can enjoy.**

The Secret of the Cards, **by Sonia Craddock, Scholastic Canada, 1990. A compelling story of time travel, ghosts, and mystery.**

Silverwing, **by Kenneth Oppel, HarperCollins, 1997. This story of a young silverwing bat and the adventures of his first migration brilliantly evokes a very different world of darkness, flight, and "echo-vision."**

Trouble on Wheels, **by Ann Aveling, Scholastic, 1994. A good little addition to the popular tradition of "kid detectives," with a fast-paced story and a surprise ending that actually makes sense.**

Your children's librarian or bookstore owner will have other good suggestions.

old. He didn't really enjoy longer books. It took me a while to realize what kind of material he liked. He was always bringing home non-fiction with lots of pictures. So we started to read more of those kinds of books."

While Sam's dad has (rather heroically) read him the entire *Lord of the Rings* trilogy twice, you don't have to subject yourself and your child to weighty classics if that's not what you both like. There's lots of great modern fiction for children, fascinating non-fiction books, and "mini-novels" that are just right for children who are ready for more sophisticated writing, but can't hang in through a full-length novel yet. Ask your children's librarian or children's bookstore owner for suggestions—and, as your child nears eight, take a look through your own bookshelves, too. Did you acquire *The Hobbit* in your student days? How about *Watership Down* or *The Little Prince?* Maybe some good science fiction? There's no point in trying adult material on children before they're ready to understand and enjoy it—but when that time comes, there's something really special about reading a book you love to your child.

Whatever you read to your beginning reader, you are giving him an experience that he can't yet provide for himself. It still takes all his attention and effort just to decode the words; when he's reading on his own there's not much room left for creative thought or aesthetic appreciation. When *you* take care of the mechanics, he can really immerse himself in the story. MacIsaac notes, "The child's mind is free to paint the pictures as he hears the story. Reading aloud allows the child to visualize, and visualizing is vital to good reading."

Another bonus: "In the oral tradition," says MacIsaac, "there is more flexibility than in reading silently." You or the child can stop at any time to ask questions, put what she hears into the larger context of the story, or relate it to her own life. If you read, "A big black bear walked by," she might stop you and ask, "Do bears live around here?" You might remember together that night you were camping, and heard something crashing through the bushes. Or she might stay in the story, and speculate, "Maybe that's the same bear that the boy saw at the beginning of the book." Then again, she might just think these things to herself, never interrupting the flow of the story but doing the "brain work" all the same.

It's great that being read to qualifies as an educational experience, but most parents and kids have a better reason for continuing the tradition: It's just a really nice way to spend time together. "Sam's at school all day, and he's a really active kid in a busy household," says his mother, Sue. "Some days, the bedtime story is the only quiet, peaceful moments we have together all day. I would hate to see that go by the boards, no matter how well he learns to read on his own."

LAST WORDS
Learning All the Time

IT WAS AN UNUSUALLY WARM SEPTEMBER DAY, and Lenore Kilmartin was driving her family to the grocery store with all the car windows open. Eight-year-old Jonathan stuck his hand out the window and held it in the breeze created by the car's motion. He noticed that when he tilted his hand slightly, the wind pressure forced it upwards. He tried tilting it in different ways. Sometimes the air pushed his hand up, other times down. And he noticed that when his mother slowed the car down, he felt less pressure against his hand.

"You know what?" he asked his mother (who had been watching all this out of the corner of her eye). "I think I just figured out how airplane wings work."

Jonathan's experience demonstrates an important fact that parents sometimes forget: Children learn an astounding amount all by themselves, without lessons, drills, or "educational" materials. The late author and education expert John Holt wrote: "Among the many things I have learned about children, learned by many, many years of hanging out with them, watching carefully what they do, and thinking about it, is that children are natural learners. The one thing we can be sure of, or surest of, is that children have a passionate desire to understand as much of the world as they can."

How can we support our children's natural desire to learn?

"My kids learn a lot just by hanging out with me," observes stay-home dad John Hoffman. "We were making cookies the other day, and the kids wanted to invent the recipe. So we did—I coached them a bit on 'essential' ingredients, and we looked at some recipes, and then they tried out their own ideas. They learned about research, experimentation, and practical baking skills, and they had a ball."

Giving kids opportunities to explore the world—not Disneyland or even the space museum necessarily, but the market, the garage, the bank, the woods, the kitchen—is a great way to encourage learning. That doesn't mean dragging bored and protesting children on every errand we do, but simply inviting them fairly often to be part of what's going on—to help choose the groceries and pay for them, to come to the vet's and observe the dog's check-up, or just to jump in the leaves while you rake. Our interest in their observations, our willingness to accommodate their curiosity ("You found a worm? Let's see. Oh, that's an inchworm—can you guess why it's called that?"), makes their learning richer.

We can also help them to follow the trail of their own interests, in a way that suits them. "By the time he was seven, it was clear that my oldest son had a great ear for music," remembers John. "But it was also clear that he wasn't ready for the structure of music lessons—he had a short attention span, and found it hard to tolerate any kind of repetitive practice. So I made myself wait until *he* wanted the lessons—at about 11. But in the meantime, I showed him a few things on my guitar and let him noodle around with it. We played lots of music at home, and went to see live performances when the opportunity arose. By the time he started lessons, he already knew a lot about music and he progressed very quickly." Books and lessons are (to adults) the most obvious routes to learning, but kids may prefer—and learn better from—a less formal approach.

Contact with people of all ages—from relatives, family friends, and classmates to the salesclerks and bus drivers we meet in our daily travels—provides an opportunity to observe and learn social skills. "We don't push them beyond their comfort zone, but we encourage our kids to speak for themselves rather than always being their go-betweens," says Lenore Kilmartin. "They are learning to become part of the wider community outside their immediate family at this age. They can line up and give their own order at Burger King, or call a museum to check on when it's open." In these days of careful streetproofing we sometimes forget the satisfaction and self-confidence children gain from learning, in the safety of their parents' presence, to communicate comfortably with all kinds of people.

Friends, of course, have a special role to play. Now and for years to come, time spent with friends is an intense growth experience, as children negotiate, argue, share, laugh, coach each other, compete, and play together. Rosemary McConnell, administrator of the Dearcroft Montessori School in Oakville, Ontario, explains that "children from age six on are at a developmental level where their social needs are paramount, and they need to have time to socialize and play freely with others."

Finally, we can value, and safeguard, our children's play. For kids, play is one of the most accessible doors into learning. "In the time that a child takes to learn one concept in reading, he or she could be developing one thousand skills through play," says Valerie Fronczek of the Vancouver Children's Play Resource Centre. "We can teach children to tie their shoes or cross the road safely—or to read. But we can't prepare them for the future, because we don't know what will happen. Only play can do that. Play helps children become more creative, more resourceful, and able to find new solutions to problems."

An inviting environment, a variety of toys, and other children to play with are valuable, but free time for playing is often the most difficult part for the child to find. If many hours of the day are already consumed by school, travelling back and forth, household chores, homework, and ballet lessons, any free time tends to be spent, exhausted, in front of the TV. Sometimes parents need to deliberately carve out free play time for their children.

John Holt's passionate plea was for parents to respect their children's natural learning style. "Children learn from anything and everything," he wrote, "... We can best help children learn, not by deciding what we think they should learn and thinking of ingenious ways to teach it to them, but by making the world, as far as we can, accessible to them."

So try to ensure that, despite the hectic pace of life, your child has time and space to just "be a kid," to play, explore, and dream. Invite her into your world frequently, and join her in hers. You may be surprised at how much *you* learn, too.

Recommended Reading

We've found the following child-rearing guides especially helpful with school-aged children:

It's Not Fair! Jeremy Spencer's Parents Let Him Stay Up All Night, by Anthony Wolfe, HarperCollins, 1995.

Kids Are Worth It: Giving Your Child the Gift of Inner Discipline, by Barbara Coloroso, Somerville House, 1994.

The Optimistic Child: A Proven Program to Safeguard Children Against Depression and Build Lifelong Resilience, by Martin E.P. Seligman, HarperPerennial, 1995.

Playground Politics: Understanding the Emotional Life of Your School-Age Child, by Stanley I. Greenspan, MD, Addison-Wesley, 1993.

Smart Parenting: An Easy Approach to Raising Happy, Well-Adjusted Kids, by Peter Favaro, Contemporary Books, 1995.

The Portable Pediatrician's Guide to Kids: Your Child's Physical and Behavioral Development from Ages 5 to 12, by Laura Walther Nathanson, MD, FAAP, HarperPerennial, 1996.

The Seven Habits of Highly Effective Families, by Stephen R. Covey, Golden Books, 1997.

Tough Questions: Talking Straight with Your Kids about the Real World, by Sheila Kitzinger and Celia Kitzinger, Harvard Common Press, 1991.